Lewisham

History and Guide

Lewisham's Jubilee Clock Tower, as sketched by the architect. The view is southwards towards the present Barclays Ban

Lewisham

History and Guide

John Coulter

ALAN SUTTON PUBLISHING LIMITED

First published in the United Kingdom in 1994
Alan Sutton Publishing Limited
Phoenix Mill · Far Thrupp · Stroud · Gloucestershire

First published in the United States of America in 1994
Alan Sutton Publishing Inc.
83 Washington Street · Dover · NH 03820

British Library Cataloguing in Publication Data

Coulter, John
Lewisham: History and Guide
I. Title
914.216304

ISBN 0-7509-0422-4

Library of Congress Cataloging-in-Publication Data applied for

Cover illustration: St Mary's church (*Stephen Moreton Pritchard*)

To Neil Rhind

Typeset in 10/13 Times.
Typesetting and origination by
Alan Sutton Publishing Limited.
Printed in Great Britain by
Ebenezer Baylis, Worcester.

Contents

1. Aliens (to 1414) 1

2. Royalty (1414–1624) 11

3. The Road to Suburbia (1624–1770) 18

4. Opulent Merchants (1770–1840) 35

5. Sewers and Steam (1840–1880) 58

6. Metropolitan Improvements? (1880–1914) 76

7. New Estates for Old (1914–1965) 92

Walking Tour: Around Lewisham 101

Map 102

Sources 111

Acknowledgements 115

Index 116

The abbey church of St Peter at Ghent, painted in 1580, shortly before rebuilding began. The abbots were lords of Lewisham for four hundred and fifty years.

CHAPTER ONE

Aliens (to 1414)

The road building activities of the Romans brought them into the outlying parts of the future parish of Lewisham, and they established settlements close to Watling Street in the north and the London–Lewes way in the west; but the founder of the village itself was probably a member of that mysterious race, the Jutes. Whether this land-hungry warrior was called Lẽof (a name meaning 'beloved'), or Lẽof-suna ('dear son'), or Lẽfsa (a nickname meaning 'crippled' or 'weak') is a point on which the experts are in their usual state of chronic disagreement, but it does seem clear that places ending in 'ham' are among the earliest of English names, suggesting that Lewisham was founded in the sixth century, and by a pagan.

The name of Lewisham is first recorded, in the form 'Liofshema', in a charter of 862, which defined the boundaries of Bromley. In 964 King Edgar described it as having been 'known to the country people from ancient usage as Lieuesham'. This serious corruption of the name by the tenth century is perhaps further evidence of early settlement, as the inhabitants clearly retained no traditional recollection of Lẽof or Lẽfsa.

The original village must have been close to the parish church of St Mary's. The first expansion would have been up and down the river valley where lay the rich meadows, the source of the village's prosperity. An early proof of this is the name 'Bellingham', which means 'the water meadow of Beora's people'. It is first recorded in 973. Quite soon, however, adventurers struck east and west into the woods. The early clearings made in the outlying parts of a 'ton' or 'ham' are often indicated by such woodland place-name endings as 'hurst' and 'ley'. The obvious example of this in Lewisham is Brockley (the area now usually called Crofton Park), although it is not recorded until the twelfth century. The place-name specialists are once more in dispute as to whether it means 'the marshy clearing' or 'Broca's clearing', but as Brockley is not on a river, the latter is perhaps more likely.

Broca and Beora (a nickname meaning 'the bear'?) may therefore be two other early Lewisham citizens, to go with Lẽof, and another is probably provided by Sydenham, or 'Cippa's settlement'.

J.K. Wallenberg has put forward the delightful theory that Cippa, or Sipa, means 'the drunkard'. The local fondness for nicknames suggests that Catford, always explained as 'the ford frequented by wild cats', may commemorate a settler known to his contemporaries as 'the cat'.

Apart from these hamlets within the parish itself it seems likely that pioneers from Lewisham also founded the communities of Mottingham, Greenwich, Woolwich and Coombe (Eastcombe, between Greenwich and Charlton), for when Lewisham first entered the field of written history in the tenth century these places were regarded as part of the manor.

The documentary history of Lewisham may well begin with a forgery. The town has long claimed Alfred as its first lord, and a medallion of the great scholar king hangs in Lewisham Library like that of a patron saint. The claim is based on a charter dated 18 September 918, by which Alfred's youngest daughter Elfrida gave to the Benedictine abbey of St Peter at Ghent (now in Belgium) 'Lewisham, Greenwich, and Woolwich, my inheritance'. In fact the estates left to Elfrida in Alfred's will were at Wellow, Ashton, and Chippenham. Elfrida was well known to the monks of St Peter's because her husband, Count Baldwin of Flanders, was buried in the abbey in 918, and she herself in 929.

Modern scholars, Belgian and English, have concluded that this 918 charter is a forgery, of a type all too sadly common in the Middle Ages. At a time when the ownership of land was frequently subject to challenge, many landlords (from the Pope downwards) sought to give added security to their titles by conjuring up documents of greater seeming age and respectability than their genuine deeds. The Abbot of Ghent's right to Lewisham was constantly disputed and required confirmation from each new king. By adding nearly fifty years to the antiquity of his title, and by attaching it to the great name of Alfred, this dubious charter may have been a valuable security to him.

If the medievalists are correct, St Peter's really gained possession of Lewisham in 964. Dunstan, later Archbishop of Canterbury, had found refuge at the abbey while exiled from England in 956. On his return home he remembered the monks' hospitality, and persuaded King Edgar to give them a reward. This was 'the place known to the country people from ancient usage as Lieuesham, with all its appurtenances, that is Grenewich, Wulleuic, Modingeham, and Cumbe'. Later in the charter there is a passage, also pronounced a forgery, recording Elfrida's donation. Without it Edgar's charter reads as a simple grant of land, not as a confirmation of an earlier gift.

ne Lewisham parish church
1764, ten years before it was
built. This sketch of the
uth elevation is the earliest
own view of St Mary's, but
certainly does not show the
st church. The architectural
tail suggests a mixture of
rteenth- and fifteenth-
ntury work, with one or two
ghteenth-century alterations.

The 964 charter mentions churches among the good things included in the manor, but the 918 document does not. Leland Duncan, trusting in its genuineness, concluded that Lewisham church was built by one of the abbots in the tenth century; but if Elfrida's gift is rejected we must suppose that the church was founded by a lay lord of the manor between the conversion of Kent to Christianity, in the seventh century, and the year 964. This accords better with the dedication to St Mary. The monks of Ghent might have been expected to name a church far from home in honour of St Peter.

Edgar's gift was potentially a very valuable one, but the king's death in 975 inaugurated a period of anarchy that culminated in Canute's seizure of the English throne in 1017. If the abbot had a prior or bailiff in Lewisham the charter of King Edgar was no protection to him against the Danes who harried Kent and London from their camp at Blackheath, and murdered Alphege, Archbishop of Canterbury, at Greenwich (where their fleet was moored) in 1012. St Peter's Abbey did not regain control of Lewisham until the reign of Edward the Confessor.

This is how Domesday Book recorded the manor of Lewisham's potential for taxation purposes in 1086:

> The land of St Peter of Ghent, in Greenwich Hundred. The Abbot of Ghent holds Levesham of the King, and he held it of King Edward. It was then, and is now, rated at two sulings. There is arable land for fourteen ploughs. There are two ploughs on the demesne land, and there are fifty villans and nine bordars, who have seventeen ploughs between them. There are three slaves. And eleven mills, with the tribute of the rustics,

> yielding eight pounds and twelve shillings. From the outgoings of the port forty shillings. There are thirty acres of meadow. Of the woods fifty hogs from the pannage. The whole was valued in King Edward's time at sixteen pounds, afterwards at twelve pounds, and now at thirty pounds.

The 'suling' was the unit by which military service, and later taxation, was assessed in Kent. The 'villans' were the principal tenants of the manor, the 'bordars' smallholders, and the 'rustics' cottagers or labourers. The 'three slaves' worked directly for the lord of the manor, cultivating the demesne lands and possibly doing the domestic work in the manor house or priory. 'Pannage' was the right to turn out pigs to graze on acorns and beech nuts in the woods in the south and east of Lewisham, and probably also in the Wealden denes at Cowden, in the south-western corner of Kent, which belonged to the manor until 1674. The 'fifty hogs' were the price paid to the abbot's representative – apparently one hog per villan – for the privilege. The 'port' was at Greenwich, where the Danish fleet had anchored earlier in the century. The increase in the number of plough teams from fourteen in Edward the Confessor's time to nineteen in 1086 indicates the speed with which woodland was being cleared, as does the rise in value from £14 to £30. From the Domesday entry Leland Duncan estimated the population of Lewisham manor (including Greenwich, and possibly Woolwich, etc.) as three to four hundred.

It is not clear how much of the extensive manor granted by King Edgar was still in the hands of the abbot. Lewisham and Greenwich certainly were, as they continued to be for centuries afterwards, and there is reason to think that he retained East Coombe; but Woolwich and Mottingham may well have been seized by William the Conqueror, for there is no doubt that his sons, William Rufus and Henry I, treated them as their own, and they make no appearance in the records of St Peter's after the Conquest.

During the anarchic years of the twelfth century the abbots were preoccupied not so much by regret for Woolwich and Mottingham as by anxiety to safeguard the remains of their estate. Several claimants came forward to dispute their rights, the most formidable being Robert of Bampton, the son of Walter of Douai, Lord of the Manor of Lee. Early in the reign of Henry I, Robert seized Lewisham and Greenwich. The dispute was taken to the king in 1109, and when Robert refused to appear before him Henry gave judgement in favour of the abbot. But in that age it was one thing to obtain a decree, quite another to enforce it. Robert and his supporters were able to cause so much trouble that the abbot eventually found it more prudent to lease the manor to him than to maintain a fruitless struggle for control. Robert's heirs were finally bought off in 1222, at the considerable cost of 101 silver marks.

It was perhaps during this period of uncertainty that the monks of Ghent decided to cut their losses by selling large parts of Lewisham in the form of subsidiary manors, freed from nearly all feudal duties. The manors thus created were Bankers (in the Brockley and Forest Hill area), Shroffold, Bellingham, Catford, and perhaps Sydenham. At the same time part of Hither Green was apparently ceded to the manor of Lee. This subinfeudation, as the practice was called, must have taken place before 1291, when it was banned by Act of Parliament.

The new owners of these estates were no doubt better able to defend themselves than was the abbot's representative. It is not known to what extent, if at all, the conflict led to actual warfare, but it is, perhaps, significant that the manor house of Lee was fortified with a moat, and that there were two moated houses at Catford, and possibly another at Ladywell. The classic era of moat construction began in about 1200, and there is evidence of a dispute over the seizure of one in Lewisham in 1205.

The abbots had not entirely abandoned the manor during this difficult century. The first known prior of Lewisham (a monk of Ghent sent over as the agent of the abbot) was Arnold, who was in residence in the years around 1167; and another prior named Sigerus is heard of during the period 1185 to 1189. After 1222 the abbots were at last able to enjoy the manor of Lewisham – or such parts of it as they retained – in comparative peace, and during the thirteenth century the list of priors is practically complete.

The house in which they lived was probably the one that had been occupied by the representatives of the abbot (whether called prior, or proctor, or bailiff) since they first came over to take control of Lewisham, and may have been the house of the earlier lords of the manor, or on its site. From an inventory among the Ghent archives, dated 1332, a fair idea of Lewisham Priory can be formed. The hall, the largest room, was the centre of the life of the house. Here meals were taken and all but the prior slept. At one end of the hall was the solar (described in the inventory as the 'room' or 'chamber'), which would have been the private apartment of the prior. There were also a chapel and a small library, a kitchen and a pantry. These were probably in wings branching from the main block, which in medieval houses usually contained only the hall and the solar. Among outbuildings ranged around the yard were a brewery, a granary and a stable.

As the priory was an important centre of Lewisham's life from as early as the tenth century until as late as the seventeenth, it is frustrating not to know where it stood. Most authorities say that it occupied the site later held by Priory Farm at Rushey Green, nearly opposite Holbeach Road, but there are grounds for thinking that this is a mistake. The name of the farm probably had a good deal to do with the belief, but it was not an ancient one. It is known from a report on the manor, made for the Abbot of Ghent in 1396, that the priory stood 'in the centre of the town of Lewisham' (source 106: II 129) which would not have been an accurate description of Priory Farm, three-quarters of a mile south of the church. Nor are there any grounds for thinking that the lord of the manor ever owned Priory Farm, which was part of the manor of Shroffold.

The origin of this dubious association is perhaps to be found in a misinterpretation of a remark by Daniel Lysons in the Kent volume of his *Environs of London*, published in 1796. He says:

> The old manor-house, which was also, as I suppose, the site of the priory, stood to the south of the church, where is now the manor-farm (source 73: IV 517).

By the time Drake and Leland Duncan came to read Lyson's work, the first farmhouse south from the church, as it had been for decades, was Priory Farm. When Lysons wrote, though, the most important part of the demesne lands in central Lewisham, the water-meadows along the Ravensbourne (now partly incorporated in Ladywell Fields), were farmed from the building immediately south of St Mary's, which was later known as Church House. It is almost certainly to this that Lysons was referring, but as there is no reason to suppose that Church House itself ever belonged to the lord of the manor, although the farmland did, this may not be the true site either.

Another possible candidate is the large Tudor mansion occupied by Sir Nicholas Stoddard in 1612. It stood on the eastern side of the High Street, in the area now graced by Albacore Crescent and the shops to its north. The Stoddards inherited their Lewisham estate from the Chesemans, who were tenants of the manor in the fifteenth and sixteenth centuries, and might have purchased the old priory at that time, and have rebuilt it.

The priors held regular manor courts at Lewisham, presumably in the priory, sometimes for Lewisham and Greenwich separately. Lewisham was divided into two parts called the Northborough and the Southborough, Greenwich into the Westborough and Eastborough. These divisions were presided over by officials elected at the manor courts, and known as Borsholders, who were responsible for bringing business to the attention of the court. This included some criminal cases, especially assaults and thefts, and such offences as encroachments on the common land and selling short measure of beer. But the primary function of the manor court was to provide income for the lord through the levying of fines and fees. The most important of these was the sum called a heriot, exacted from the heir of a dead tenant before he could succeed to the estate. This feudal version of death duty was often paid in kind. In Lewisham 'an ox worth one mark' was sometimes the rate.

The over-zealous collection of fees and dues was one of the many points on which the priors found themselves in dispute with their tenants, but these arguments, conducted in a civilized way, were untypical of medieval Lewisham. Murders were common, and the priors must have noted with concern that the victims were often men of the church. In the first few years of the reign of Henry III, Nicholas, pastor of Lewisham, was 'found slain on a heath in Lewisham', and Martin, 'a certain friar of East Strafford' was arrested for the crime (source 28: pp. 280–1); 'Henry, a chaplain, was slain in a certain chapel at Lewisham'; and another priest was 'found in the vill of Brockley killed by persons unknown'. Not that the laity were any safer. In 1278 'Matthew de Pontefract and James son of Henry de Brocole met in the vill of Lewisham and quarrelled. Henry [*sic*] struck Matthew with a club so that he died the same night.' Blackheath was as dangerous then as it continued to be until the nineteenth century, and the 'certain merchant . . . killed by malefactors unknown at Blackhatfeuld' had at least the comfort of being one of many. On the rare occasions when a suspect was arrested, he or she might be placed in the prior of Lewisham's prison, but this seems to have been as little escape-proof as any

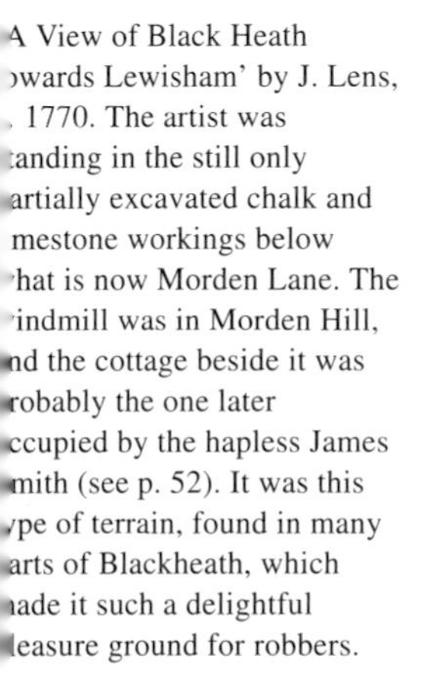

A View of Black Heath
›wards Lewisham' by J. Lens,
. 1770. The artist was
:anding in the still only
artially excavated chalk and
mestone workings below
'hat is now Morden Lane. The
'indmill was in Morden Hill,
nd the cottage beside it was
robably the one later
ccupied by the hapless James
mith (see p. 52). It was this
ype of terrain, found in many
arts of Blackheath, which
ıade it such a delightful
leasure ground for robbers.

modern gaol. Most murderers 'fled the realm', either directly or via their prisons.

The most serious of the many problems faced by the priors of Lewisham during the later Middle Ages was the result of international politics. The long series of Anglo–French wars fostered chauvinism, and after the expulsion of the Jews, the eyes of hard-pressed kings and parliaments were turned increasingly on the foreign-owned priories and their estates. Here were both scapegoats – alien monks sending money and intelligence overseas to frustrate the efforts of our brave armies – and an easy solution to the problem of war finance.

The first king to seize the estates of the 'alien religious of the power of the King of France and his allies' was Edward I, in 1295. He also ordered that all the monks from priories near to the sea or navigable rivers should be sent inland. Jean de Brean, the Prior of Lewisham, was an object of particular suspicion as the master of the port of Greenwich, and he was placed under religious house arrest at Oxford.

The alien priories were soon restored to their owners, but the damaging precedent had been set and was followed with increasing frequency during the fourteenth century. Lewisham was several times in the hands of Edward II, and during the long French wars of Edward III, the Abbey of Ghent rarely had control of the manor. In 1337 an Act of Parliament forbad the alien priories to send any money to their parent houses abroad. Lewisham was seized again, although the prior was allowed to remain as custodian of the manor for the king. He agreed to pay an annual rent of ten marks to the exchequer, but was unable to do so. Thus began an unhappy period when bailiffs of the modern kind became regular callers at Lewisham Priory (and found less of value to seize on each visit), as the priors struggled to cope with the demands of the king and of various private creditors.

When the possessions of the alien priories were restored in 1361, after the Treaty of Bretigny had brought the war to a temporary halt, it might have been expected that the position of the abbot and his prior would improve; but during the decades in which communication between Ghent and Lewisham had been practically impossible, the Black Death had swept across Europe, reaching England in 1348, and killing an estimated third, or even half, of the population. Its effects in the Hundred of Blackheath are most dramatically seen in the case of Kidbrooke, which is generally supposed to have been entirely wiped out by the plague. In Lewisham itself it has been plausibly suggested (by Mr Godfrey Smith) that the hamlet of Romborough suffered the same fate. This settlement, corresponding roughly to the modern Hither Green, was one of the most important in Lewisham during the early Middle Ages, and de Romborough was a very common local surname, but both the hamlet and the name vanish from the records after the middle of the fourteenth century, except in the form of Romborough Lane or Romborough Forest. In September 1348 the churches of Lewisham and Greenwich were reported to be without clergy and practically derelict, though it is unclear whether this was the result of the plague or of the general difficulties of the prior. What is certain is that the Black Death reduced the value of even efficiently run manors by greatly increasing the cost of labour and by accelerating the decline of the traditional feudal services. The extent to which the Abbot of Ghent was hit by these economic woes of the land-owning classes is revealed by a survey of the manor carried out for the king in 1370, showing it to be valueless except for a few small rents and dues.

The Peasants' Revolt of 1381, partly caused by the efforts of Parliament to limit the wages of labourers, could not fail to affect Lewisham, because Wat Tyler, Jack Straw and their supporters camped on Blackheath before their march to London. At that time Lewisham Hill had wide stretches of common land on either side of the roadway, extending Blackheath down to the High Street. It is not certain that there was a prior in residence in that year. If there was, his life must have been in great danger, as two particular objects of the rebels' hatred were foreigners and ecclesiastical landlords.

By this time the income of the alien priories was perhaps regarded as an integral part of the royal revenues, for their estates were in the hands of the king during most of the reigns of Richard II and Henry IV. They served the double purpose of providing cash and creating offices (custodian of this or that priory) with which to reward or appease courtiers. The long anticipated end to the Abbey of Ghent's 450 year association with Lewisham came in 1414, when the renewal of the French war led Parliament to petition Henry V to expel all foreign monks and to confiscate their possessions. He was not hard to persuade.

The rule of the abbots of Ghent as lords of the manor of Lewisham appears like a chronicle of disasters. To conclude that such was the case would certainly be an exaggeration, for history must be written from the records that survive, and the years in which the revenues of Lewisham flowed peacefully to Flanders will have produced far fewer documents than those in which they were interrupted. Nevertheless, the story of the manor during the Middle Ages is not one of success or prosperity. But because of the wise determination of the abbots to make money from Lewisham while

Place House (another of the great medieval houses of Lewisham), as drawn by J.C. Barrow in 1791. It had been partially demolished about te years earlier. Lists of the lords of the manor of Catford start with the Abel family. This is perhaps a mistake, as in 1319 John Abel obtained permissio to divert the road from Catfor to Beckenham so as to enlarg his house at Sydenham. This seems to mean Place House, which was the manor house o Sydenham, not Catford.

they could, the problems of the chief manor directly affected less and less of Lewisham as the centuries passed. In the subsidiary manors, which accounted for three-quarters or more of the parish, there is every reason to believe that population and wealth were growing, as more of the woodlands were cleared for cultivation. Wool was then the great staple of English export, and much of the new land was given over to sheep farming, which retained a central place in Lewisham's agriculture at least until the middle of the seventeenth century, though later it was of less importance.

Outside Lewisham village itself the chief medieval houses of which we have some record were in and around Catford. The manor house almost certainly occupied the moat which survived until the nineteenth century just to the east of Catford Bridge station. Later this was the site of the manor farm, which in 1806 was converted into a villa called Ravensbourne Lodge. The other Catford moat, at Priory Farm on the east side of Rushey Green, probably belonged originally to the great mansion called Rushey Green Place. This house is not heard of after the early seventeenth century, and Priory Farm was thought to have been built before 1700.

CHAPTER TWO

Royalty (1414–1624)

Royal interest in north-western Kent had been increasing during the later Middle Ages. In the fourteenth century, and perhaps earlier, kings had lived occasionally at the Moated House, on the borders of Rotherhithe and Deptford. Edward II and his successors made Eltham Palace a favourite residence, and in the early fifteenth century attention was about to shift to Greenwich, which still remained a part of the manor of Lewisham. In these circumstances it is surprising that in 1415, only a year after Lewisham fell into his hands, Henry V should have given it to his newly founded Carthusian priory of Shene, in Surrey. The manor thus remained for over a century more in the possession of absentee ecclesiastical lords, but nevertheless Lewisham was now very much within the royal orbit. The kings of the House of Lancaster, as founders of Shene Priory, clearly felt free to deal with its property much as they liked.

Late in the fourteenth century Blackheath had begun its long career as a venue for national pageantry, and during the fifteenth the mayor and aldermen and citizens of London were constantly riding out to greet their kings, and their kings' royal visitors, on this natural parade ground. Within a few years the emperors of both the east and the west were met here with great ceremony, before being led into the capital; and in 1518 the Papal Legate, Cardinal Campeggio, was entertained by William Hatcliffe, or Hattecliff, at Rushey Green Place, on his way to a state reception on the Heath.

During the Wars of the Roses, and their stormy prelude and aftermath, Blackheath was often the scene of less happy events, which must have had repercussions in Lewisham itself. In 1450 Jack Cade emulated Wat Tyler by assembling his rebels here for a month or more before marching on London. After his defeat and death, many of his followers walked back to Blackheath to beg, on their knees, for a pardon from Henry VI. In 1452 the king returned with his own army to overawe the Duke of York, who was encamped with his supporters near Dartford. Lewisham's only battle was fought on the Heath in 1497, when some six thousand Cornish rebels, protesting against heavy taxation, were massacred by Henry VII's army. It is probable that Whitefield's Mount covers the grave of the heroic Cornishmen, so that it might be described as a shrine not only of Methodism, but of tax evasion.

Apart from these stirring national events the rule of Shene Priory was uneventful. In the early years there was a bitter legal struggle with the abbots of Ghent, who were unwilling to accept the loss of the manor and sought papal assistance. The monks of Shene were probably more worried by the threat from an infinitely stronger opponent than the Pope – the Vicar of Lewisham, who in 1420 claimed part of the tithes as his own and collected them by force. This dispute was only ended, by a compromise, in 1431.

There is no evidence of contributions from Shene to any local projects or causes, so there was probably little sympathy for the prior when, in 1518, Henry VIII attempted to deprive him of the manor of Lewisham by a despicable piece of legal chicanery. The king's lawyers argued that as Lewisham had been given to Shene by Henry V, a usurping Lancastrian, the grant was null and void, and the manor still the property of the Crown. Luckily the prior was able to produce a confirmation which his far-seeing predecessor had obtained from Edward IV, the immaculate Yorkist. Henry was thus foiled for the time being, but his attachment to his birthplace, and plans for his favourite palace there, urged him to the uncharacteristic resource of persuasion. In 1531 the Prior of Shene was induced to exchange Lewisham and Greenwich for lands in Buckinghamshire, which rapidly returned to the king's hands at the Dissolution.

Henry's interest was with Greenwich, which after perhaps nine hundred years was now effectively separated from Lewisham. The stewardship became an office to be competed for by the courtiers of Henry and his successors. There were consolation prizes too, such as a farmership of the rectory or a keepership of Westwood Common.

In the century during which Lewisham remained a royal manor it clearly saw something of its masters and mistresses. Henry VIII continued the tradition of Blackheath pageantry when he staged a magnificent entertainment there in 1540 to welcome Anne of Cleves, his imported wife. Edward VI and Elizabeth also used the Heath for exercise and display, and the queen had the measure of the village itself, to judge from her traditional description of it as 'long, lazy, lousy Lewisham'. It was a popular place of residence for minor courtiers under the Tudors and the first two Stuarts, and this occasionally led to a royal visit. John Chamberlain relates that in 1602, 'on Mayday the Queen went a mayenge to Sir Richard Buckley's at Lewisham, some three or fowre miles of Greenwich' (source 28: p. 252, n. 9). Her host was Sir Richard Bulkeley of Beaumaris, and the spot where the maying party picnicked has been identified since at least 1719 with Honor Oak Hill, so named in commemoration of the event. The Bulkeleys lived at Sydenham. James I's estimate of Lewisham, more practical and Scottish than Elizabeth's, has been recorded by Francis Bacon.

> As he was going through Lusen, by Greenwich, he asked 'what town it was?' They said, 'Lusen.' He asked a good while after, 'What town is this we are now in?' They said still 'twas Lusen. 'On my soul,' said the king, 'I will be king of Lusen' (source 34: I 20).

The peremptory Tudors treated Lewisham as if it were their home farm. Queen Elizabeth would order the constable of Lewisham to collect from his fellow parishioners 'forty full lodes of good and freshe haye' (source 67: PT 84/498), and deliver them to Greenwich Palace; in 1545 Henry VIII sold the part of Westwood, or Sydenham, Common on which Honor Oak Road and its offshoots are now built; and Edward VI and Elizabeth felled the Westwood timber and carted it to Deptford to be turned into warships. Henry's sale was quite illegal, as Westwood was common pasture land, in which all the people of Lewisham had rights. But where was the man brave enough to tell him so? When James I tried to emulate Henry it was to be quite a different matter.

[…]e tower of St Mary's, as […]pleted by William […]nerig in about 1500, drawn […]rtly before it was altered […]ing the 1770s' rebuilding of […] body of the church. For […]turies this was the tallest […]cture in the parish, and […]ble from most parts of it, […] today it is the oldest […]hitectural relic in […]visham.

For while owners and their agents came and went the people of Lewisham – most of them cottagers or small farmers – were forming a community with a fair measure of local patriotism and pride. The parish rather than the manor began to be the rallying point. In the 1470s it had become the fashion (encouraged, no doubt, by weekly exhortations from the vicar) for wealthy residents to make bequests for the upkeep either of the church or of the highways. Some left money to repair the road between their own houses and the church; the more altruistic remembered 'the making of the bridge at the north end of the town of Lewisham', or 'the causey at Catford'. The parish also had almshouses for the support of its aged poor. The great communal effort of the fifteenth century was the building (or perhaps more likely the rebuilding) of the tower of St Mary's church. Between 1471 and 1529 nearly every Lewisham will contained a bequest (of sums ranging from 3s. to 26s. 8d.) for the works on the 'campanile' or 'stepill', or for the windows and bells. Even so, the project ran into trouble and precipitated the first financial scandal in the history of Lewisham's local government. The churchwarden in about 1500, one William Grenerig, thought he had secured the agreement of his wealthier fellow parishioners to pay for the completion of the tower, and in that trust called 'to him masons, carpenters, and other men such as were necessary for the bylding of the same steple and by there advyces fynyshed and made an ende of the seid steple' at his own 'costys' (source 31: p. 4). But on his requesting the contributions of his neighbours they one and all refused to pay. When he was dying in 1505 Grenerig pointedly desired to be buried in the adjoining parish of Lee.

From the middle of the sixteenth century Lewisham was fortunate in possessing a number of good vicars, who fostered the local spirit and directed it into new paths. John Glynn, who served from 1546 until 1568, left £100 for the creation of a grammar school in the parish, and this foundation received a charter from Queen Elizabeth in 1574. The master in the mid-1570s was perhaps the Huguenot refugee Claudius Hollyband, who certainly kept a school 'at Lewsham, hard by the church' (source 52: p. xvi), and was honoured there by a visit from the queen. He mentions in *The French Schoolemaister* that the captain of the school, Henry Edmoundes, 'did pronounce an Oration before the Queenes majestie, when she was now of late at Lewsham' (source 14: p. 34). (Mr Robert Edmundes of Sydenham was one of the original governors of Glynn's foundation.) Lewisham could scarcely have supported two schools. Indeed, one soon proved too much of a burden, and Glynn's had faded to almost nothing when it was revived by Abraham Colfe in the next century.

From 1596 until 1610 the vicar was Adrian de Saravia, another French refugee. He had an influence on the development of the English language as one of the translators of the authorized version of the Bible – it is curious to speculate on which of its famous phrases were first committed to paper at the old vicarage of St Mary's – but his chief gift to the parish was his choice of Abraham Colfe as his curate and eventual successor.

Colfe's first important work began in 1605, only a year after he arrived in the parish. 'Henry Newport of Lewisham, gentleman, and yeoman of ye boiling-house to King James' (source 29: p. 16), searching hungrily, as courtiers had always done, for a scrap to beg from his master's table, chose Westwood, one of the two great commons of the parish of Lewisham. Newport persuaded the king to regard this morsel of five or six hundred acres, now covered by much of Forest Hill and Upper Sydenham, as part of the demesne land of the manor, and in that belief James leased Westwood to him.

Most of the inhabitants of Lewisham were still small farmers and husbandmen. Exclusive of the demesne lands there were during that period only eleven farms over twenty-five acres and only three over one hundred. The most common size of agricutural unit was five or ten acres. Smallholdings of this kind relied heavily on the free pasture available at Sydenham. In many parishes where commons were small a rationing system was applied, whereby freeholders were entitled to keep only a specified number of cows and sheep and pigs on the common in proportion to the size of their estates. But Westwood was so big that no restrictions were applied. This had encouraged large numbers of squatters to build cottages at Sydenham, where they supported themselves almost entirely by grazing animals. In one of the petitions, which 'the inhabitants of the Parrishe of Lewsham' now fired off in all directions, they pointed out (probably with considerable exaggeration) that there were 'above 500 poore housholders with wives and manye children greatly relieved by the sayde Common and would be utterly undone yf yt should be unjustly taken from them' (source 29: p. 18). If that had happened their support would have become the responsibility of the parish, which no doubt helps to explain why the opposition to Newport was so generously supported by the richest landowners in Lewisham. On one occasion 'the mayor and cominalty of ye cytye of London' (as owners of the Bridge House estates) paid £70, and Sir Charles Howard of Rushey Green Place the staggering sum of £170 (source 20).

Three years of legal manoeuvring ended inconclusively in 1608. In 1614 (by which time Colfe was the vicar) Newport acquired two allies in Robert Raynes, sergeant of the buckhounds, and Innocent Lanier of Greenwich, one of the eminent family of court musicians, and jointly with them took a new sixty year lease from the king of 347 acres of Westwood at a rent of forty marks a year. 'Presently,' Colfe noted, 'the Patentees began to make ditches about the common and inclosed it and drave out and killed sundry of the cattell of the inhabitants' (source 29: p. 19). There were violent scenes at Sydenham when the more hot-headed parishioners levelled the ditches and broke down the new gates; and Lanier's servant responded by driving off the animals pastured on the common, killing some in the process, and by burning the furze that the poor people used for fuel.

On 20 October 1614 Colfe adopted a more peaceful approach by leading a deputation of:

> neer 100 people young and old . . . through ye city of London and a little on this side of Topnam high-crosse petitioned King James who very graciously heard ye petition and ordered the Lords of his Privy Counsell should take a course that he might be no more troubled about it (source 29: p. 19).

There were still several legal setbacks to overcome, but with the king anxious to avoid trouble on the politically sensitive question of enclosures, the final verdict was given in favour of the inhabitants of Lewisham at the end of 1615.

One of the many documents that survive from this long and wordy dispute is 'The humble petition of the poor inhabitants of Lewisham in Kent' (source 20) to the Lord Chief Baron of the Exchequer and his brethren. One hundred and forty-five names are subscribed, but only Colfe and twelve other petitioners were able to sign, and several of those did so in a laboured manner which suggests they could write little else. This may have directed Colfe's thoughts towards education, another field in which he was to do valuable work for the parish.

In 1610, while the great Westwood dispute was still continuing, another crisis arose. Sir Nicholas Stoddard (one of an extraordinary feuding family, the annals of which would provide material for any number of historical romances) had been a generous supporter of the Westwood defence fund, but that did not save him from the accusation of threatening another of the poor parishioners' common rights. He insisted on driving his cattle across the half-year land of South Field (now Lewisham Park), which he could not do without devastating the autumn crop of peas and the like which his humble neighbours had a right to grow there. After some angry confrontations in the High Street Sir Nicholas was eventually able to prove his right of way, in a case which demonstrated the fragile nature of the solidarity of rich and poor established during the Westwood dispute.

Sir Nicholas had a more positive influence on the affairs of Lewisham through his wood-felling activities. He obtained his Lewisham estates through intermarriage with the Cheseman family, who were, among other things, timber merchants on a large scale. They had cleared a great extent of woodland in Lewisham, especially in the Sydenham area, during the years in which they leased the manor from the priors of Shene, and Stoddard continued their work along the thickly forested ridge that divided Lewisham from Lee. In the characteristic fashion of his family he made no bones about breaking covenants. The Hither Green estate which he leased from Trinity Hospital, Greenwich, he proceeded, as they complained, to convert without authorization 'from good woodland to ill pasture' (source 28: p. 193, n. 1).

By the beginning of the seventeenth century the work of the Chesemans, the Stoddards and many others had given the parish the outline of settlement it was to retain with little change for nearly two hundred years. The village of Lewisham itself was much the most populous, with an irregular scattering of houses stretching from the bridge southwards nearly to the modern George Lane. Next in importance was Sydenham, which had grown from its origins in Perry Hill down to Sydenham (now Bell) Green, and then westwards

. View of Brookley in Kent', ıblished by Carrington ›wles in 1771. It almost ɾtainly depicts the hamlet of 'ockley in Lewisham, now ɔre often thought of as ›ofton Park, for Brockley in ɘptford then comprised only o isolated farms.

along Sydenham Road to the common. Apart from these there were only the villages or hamlets of Southend, Brockley and Catford, and a few scattered farms. The biggest houses were near the church, and at Catford, where Rushey Green Place was the property of the beautiful and imperious Mary Fitz, the Wife of Lewisham, who outwitted and outlived four husbands.

James I made the greatest possible political use of the manor by granting a vast array of leases, patents, reversions, and fee-farm rents. The lucky courtiers then sub-let their various interests until the situation grew quite bewildering. Two famous men thus became involved in the fortunes of Lewisham. From 1604 the king delegated his powers as lord of the manor to no less a person than Sir Robert Cecil, Earl of Salisbury, chief minister to James as he had been to Elizabeth. Later there was a brief theatrical interlude when the great actor Edward Alleyn, the founder of Dulwich College, bought the office of 'his Majesty's farmer of the manor of Lewisham'. On 11 December 1620 he recorded in his diary that 'I was in London with Sir Jo. Wildgosse about the manor of Lewisham' and on the 15th that 'This day I paid for the maner and parsonage of Lewisham £1,000' (source 21: p. 163). He held his first manor court on 16 April 1621, and we may guess that he directed the proceedings with more style than any of his predecessors or successors.

Having thoroughly complicated the situation, the king decided to leave it to someone else to unravel. In 1624 he gave all his rights in the manor to his Scottish favourite John Ramsay, Earl of Holderness, and the royal connection with Lewisham was broken for ever.

CHAPTER THREE

The Road to Suburbia (1624–1770)

Superficially, the century and a half covered by this chapter may not seem a period of great change or of vital significance. The population of Lewisham was probably not far from one thousand during most of the seventeenth century. (From the Compton Census of 1676 an estimate of 983 may be arrived at. There were 550 adult conformists to only 40 adult non-conformists.) Its rise was checked by the last three great outbreaks of plague, which raised the average annual death rate of thirty or so to 117 in 1603, 103 in 1625, 56 in 1665 and 52 in 1666. Thereafter the population rose, to about 1,500 in 1730, and 2,700 in 1770. This was a sharp jump in forty years, but trivial by comparison with what was to come in the next forty. Despite the near tripling of the population in the period now under review, the obvious physical changes in the parish were surprisingly light. The only new settlement was the luxurious one on Blackheath. The rest of the newcomers were accommodated by squeezing more houses into the existing villages, especially in the High Street, and at Sydenham, where the population more than doubled between 1730 and 1770.

Beneath the surface, however, fundamental changes were taking place. In 1624 the typical Lewisham citizen was the illiterate owner or tenant of a small farm. By 1770 the farmers and farm labourers were only one group (and a declining one) out of four that dominated the parish. The others were the manufacturers and their workmen; the merchants and professional men, active and retired; and the tradesmen who catered to the needs of the wealthy. It is hard to draw sharp distinctions between these groups. Many labourers doubtless worked alternately in agriculture or industry as the opportunities arose; some retired merchants became farmers; some farmers were also shopkeepers. What is certain is that the numbers of farmers, and their influence upon parish affairs, were both in decline.

Woodland in the south of Lewisham was still being cleared, but the farmland gained there was cancelled by that lost in the north, where more and more was required for the parks and gardens of the wealthy new inhabitants. At the same time there was a strong tendency for the size of farms to increase. The surviving farmers grew wealthy, educated their children, and identified more with the middle class settlers, leaving the farm labourers to sink further into poverty.

All this was latent in the early seventeenth century, when Lewisham found itself with an absentee lord of the manor. The title passed rapidly between several short-lived members of the Ramsay family, none of whom made any recorded mark on Lewisham life. In 1640 the manor was bought by Raynold (or Reginald) Grahme, a London draper, whose chief estates and interests were in Yorkshire. He was childless, and in 1673 conveyed Lewisham to his nephew George Legge, later Lord Dartmouth. It was only from about 1690, when Dartmouth's son came to live for part of the year at Blackheath, that the affairs of the manor began to be closely supervised by its lord. In 1624 the parish turned for leadership to Abraham Colfe.

Leadership was sorely needed in the dangerous times that were approaching. The simple farmers of Lewisham seem to have been willing to accept with perfect equanimity whatever doctrines were handed down from the pulpit. There is no record of the rapid religious alterations of the sixteenth century provoking the slightest dissent. But the village was changing. In the 1630s and '40s an influential minority of merchants and lawyers from London had gathered in Lewisham, and some of these early suburbanites were deeply infected with the poisonous puritanical doctrines then so prevalent in the City. Colfe's opinions were clearly moderate and sensible, and inevitably the target for violent abuse.

The puritan campaign in Lewisham began with a great many prosecutions of innkeepers for allowing such wicked and demoralizing games as shovegroate to be played in their pubs. In 1630 there was embarrassment for Colfe when Thomas Hurles of Lewisham, victualler, was accused of having 'on 31 January . . . being the Sabbath . . . allowed Roger Whitlocke and William Grove and his wife, all servants of Abraham Colfe, of Lewisham, clerk, to be drinking in his house at the time of divine service'. The same innkeeper was also charged with having 'entertained in his house two servants of Richard Valentyne, Churchwarden of Lewisham, until an unlawful time of night, last winter, and allowed one of them to become drunk, and when Richard Valentyne sent another servant for them, he kept him there for an hour and more after nine at night' (source 67: PT 67/6). Richard Valentine was Colfe's stepson.

These were only skirmishes. With the opening of the Long Parliament at the end of 1640 the puritans were emboldened to

'A View at Lewisham, in Kent' published by Carringt Bowles in 1770. This is the oldest known picture of a Lewisham inn, but which is If the water in the foregroun can be identified as the High Street stream, then the pub w on the west side of the road. That might make it a forerunner of The George, which was built in its preser form in about 1800, on the s of some old farm buildings. Farms often doubled as pubs

proceed to more violent measures. They had been deeply offended by Archbishop Laud's order that communion tables should be moved to the east end of churches and protected by railings from irreverent use. This order was thought to smack of Roman Catholicism, although the strong anti-papist Colfe made no bones about obeying. The conscripts raised in the south-eastern counties for the Scottish war, many of them puritans, now began to deal with the matter in their own way. Their doings were recorded with relish by Nehemiah Wallington, a fanatical parishioner of Colfe's at his other parish, St Leonard, Eastcheap:

> Of the exploits that I heere very credably that the solgars did in Kent. At Lusame, the 9 January [1641] being Satterday at night when they were ringing the belles, the Railes that ware about the Communion Tabel ware pulled up, and not knowen who did it, nor what became of them, as it is thought they were cast into the river and so carried quite away (source 29: p. 42).

('Lusame' was a common spelling of Lewisham at that time, and indicates the old pronunciation.)

In 1642, with the situation tending rapidly towards open hostilities between the king and Parliament, Colfe himself was attacked on several fronts. The Commons had begun to appoint puritan lecturers to parishes where the vicar was considered inactive, or of royalist sympathies. The opposition party in Lewisham applied for one, and on 26 February it was ordered that:

> Mr John Batchelor, an orthodox divine, be appointed Lecturer, to preach every Tuesday in the week in the Parish of Lewisham; the inhabitants of the said Parish allowing him a competent maintenance for the same; and

> Mr Abraham Colfe, Vicar of the said Parish, is hereby required to permit the said Mr Batchelor the free use of his pulpit, to preach there every Tuesday as aforesaid (source 29: pp. 42–3).

John Batchelor duly came to Lewisham, but his lectures were so effectively boycotted by the loyal majority of Colfe's congregation that in 1643 he organized a new petition to complain that his work 'has been much molested and hindered by Mr Abraham Colfe, the vicar, and some of the parishioners'. Despite obtaining a confirmation of his appointment, Batchelor could never establish himself in Lewisham and eventually withdrew. In his will Colfe sadly remembered how some of his flock, 'at the instigation of their impudent Lecturer . . . articled against me to the honorable Committee for plundered ministers, and endeavoured to have deprived me of the Benefit of my Vicarage . . .' (source 29: p. 43).

In the same year Colfe was forced to resign his living of St Leonard, Eastcheap. As some mitigation of this loss, Colfe may have expected that it would free him from the attentions of Nehemiah Wallington, but in August he was pursued to Lewisham by a long letter of abuse from 'your loving parishioner that was'. It throws a lurid light on the troubles of Lewisham at this time:

> And shurely, Sir, I am perswaded if you had privately and publikly told your people plainly of their wicked wayes . . . (you having so long lived at Lusume as you have done) then shurely there would not have bine so many ignorant, Drunken, Swearers, Mockers and profainers of the Lords Day at Lusume as now there be. I did here one say that it is as rude and profaine a place as ever they did know which doth much abound in your old days to your discredit.
>
> When I was at your Towne on Lector Day, there was a woman swore a grevious oth that there was a Lector at their Church, but shee said shee was never at it: nor never would be. And hard by your Church as soune as Lector was done what roreing in the alehouse, mocking and calling of Roundhead, and I did here that there were some such in your house. Nay was not there swilling in the alehouse when others were hearing of Gods word, and I was tould by a stranger that awhile after there was three drunke, he meet them himselfe in a lettel space of your house.
>
> Can these sinnes abound in your Towne and you not know of it, and if you know it can you not helpe itt. O then call in more helpe, some more faithful minister to preach and cry down these sinnes and abominations which cry for Gods judgments which now are coming upon us amaine. O I cannot but lament the wickednesse of Lusame . . . (source 29: p. 46).

From all this it is clear that the majority supported Colfe's moderate royalism and Anglicanism, but the inhabitants of a village so near to London could not avoid obedience to the parliamentary line in politics or religion, especially after large numbers of troops were billeted on them in 1643 and 1644. They were partly there to enforce payment of the 'voluntary' contributions required by the Commons. This was another way of striking at covert opponents like Colfe, and he was assessed at £100, although he managed never to pay more than £75. These exactions were often described (with unexpected humour) as 'loans', and in his will Colfe optimistically urged his executors to press for repayment.

Colfe must have compromised to the extent of signing the Solemn League and Covenant in 1644. This enabled him to retain his church and to continue his ambitious schemes for the good of the parish; and even after the use of the prayer book was forbidden in 1645, he was able to conduct services of a kind acceptable to his Anglican congregation. The ministers of most neighbouring parishes had been ejected in favour of puritans, so John Evelyn of Deptford was one royalist, probably of many, who came to hear Colfe. In February 1652, he records:

> I went to Leusham where I heard an honest sermon . . . This was the first Sonday I had ben at Church since my returne [from France], it being now a very rare thing to find a Priest of the Church of England in a Parish pulpet, most of them fill'd with Independents & Phanatics (source 36: III 60).

These political troubles interfered seriously with the great charitable tasks that Colfe had set himself. Glynn's school had limped on in some form into the seventeenth century, but its financial position was fatally weak, and Colfe decided to re-found it on a secure basis. Some of the land he acquired in the Perry Hill area as an endowment was next to a charitable estate administered by the Leathersellers. It was probably this that induced Colfe to approach the company in 1634 and ask them to act as his trustees and bankers. Colfe's schemes were approaching completion in the late 1630s, but everything was thrown into confusion by the outbreak of the Civil War. The loss of income from his other parish, and the money he had to pay to the House of Commons, prevented Colfe from adding to the endowments. In 1648 he was forced to write to the Leathersellers to request them to pay five per cent interest on his money, because of 'the hardness of the times'.

The centre-piece of Colfe's charities was his grammar school, which he designed for the good of the Hundred of Blackheath. In 1650 he persuaded the lord of the manor to grant him a piece of waste land on the east side of Lewisham Hill. The school was built there in 1651 and opened in June 1652. Colfe appointed as the first master the Revd Matthew Day, a royalist who had been ejected from his parish of Everdon in Northants.

The grammar school was intended primarily for the children of 'ordinary people', and to prepare them for its classical syllabus Colfe had already opened an English or reading school in the High Street. (It was to close after being made redundant by the 1870 Education Act, and its site is now covered by part of the hospital.) To complete his comprehensive scheme of education Colfe established seven university scholarships, and a public library at the grammar school for the further education of the district.

In addition to his educational charities Colfe left funds for several annual gifts to the poor, and for the building of a set of almshouses for five parishioners aged sixty or over. He died in 1657, and the Leathersellers built the five almshouses (plus a sixth at their own expense) between 1663 and 1665. Colfe's school and almshouses remain as a memorial to the generous founder, although neither is in its original building or on its original site, and the school has sadly migrated to the borough of Greenwich.

The second half of the seventeenth century was a period of improvement in Lewisham. The parish had long provided a home for wealthy men whose income was not earned, or acquired, there. First had come the minor courtiers and royal hangers-on from Greenwich, and then the lawyers and merchants from London. With the tendency for farms to increase in size there had been enough abandoned farmhouses to satisfy this moderate demand for country retreats. It was only now that an attempt was made to attract settlers by the offer of new accommodation.

This probably happened first in Sydenham. At the time of the Westwood Common dispute, between 1605 and 1615, the village had consisted of a collection of prosperous farms in Perry Hill and around Sydenham (later Bell) Green, and a great many small cottages stretching along Sydenham Road to the fringes of the common. Because the Great North Wood formed such a solid barrier to the west, Upper Sydenham was then the most remote, backward, and impoverished settlement in Lewisham.

Things began to change in the 1640s, when the medicinal properties of certain springs on Westwood Common were first noticed by the world in general. The village was then so obscure that the spa came to be generally called Dulwich Wells, from the nearest place widely known to the Londoners. By 1651 the flood of summer visitors to Sydenham was so great that the government issued a proclamation ordering them to behave with decorum. When this did no good, cavalry was sent to maintain order. Evelyn visited the wells in 1675 and noted that they were 'much frequented in Summer time' (source 36: IV 74). Daniel Defoe was another visitor (before 1724), and he relates how:

we turn'd away by Beckenham, and thro' Norwood to Croydon; in the Way we saw Dullige or Sydenham Wells, where great Crouds of People throng every Summer from London to drink the Waters, as at Epsome and Tunbridge; only with this difference, that as at Epsome and Tunbridge, they go more for the Diversion of the Season, for the Mirth and the Company; for Gaming, or Intrieguing, and the like, here they go for meer Physick, and this causes another difference; Namely, that as the Nobility and Gentry go to Tunbridge, the Merchants and Rich Citizens to Epsome; so the Common People go chiefly to Dullwich and Stretham; and the rather also, because it lyes so near London, that they can walk to it in the Morning, and return at Night; which abundance do; that is to say, especially of a Sunday, or on Holidays, which makes the better sort also decline the Place; the Croud on those Days being both unruly and unmannerly (source 24: 2nd pag., p. 107)).

An early attempt was apparently made 'by the instigation of a forward and active person' to enclose and monopolize the waters, and a handsome well was dug, but:

no sooner was the well finished, though supplied with water very plentifully, but it lost its taste, its odour, and effects; which was so manifestly observable that thereupon there was immediately a final end put to that specious project . . . (source 18: p. 9).

After this fiasco the profits arising from entertaining the visitors at the various wells (near the junction of the present Taylor's Lane and Wells Park Road), and at the houses near the common, were fairly widely diffused among the residents. This must have raised the standard of living, and certainly led to an improvement in the quality of Sydenham's houses. The fine ones that still survive in Sydenham Road are typical of many that were built in the village late in the seventeenth century, perhaps primarily to lodge the water drinkers.

The proprietors of the variou[s] wells at Sydenham built cottages for their own accommodation, and the entertainment of the water drinkers. The Green Dragon ('the dwelling of Alexander Roberts') was the most celebrated of them, and survived the longest, only succumbing to a German bo[mb] in 1944. Its site is marked b[y] the curve of Oaksford Aven[ue] at its junction with Wells Pa[rk] Road.

Not that they confined themselves to water. From an early period there were complaints that some visitors took 'an excess quantity of brandy or other strong liquors, thereby many of them becoming greatly prejudiced in their health (to add to their folly and crime) have not been ashamed to impute their indisposition to this water'. It all turned to the profit of the residents, and it seems likely that the earliest Sydenham public houses were built, in part at least, for the convenience of the visitors to the wells.

Their spiritual welfare worried one Mrs Quicke, the widow of a Nonconformist minister, who in 1706 and 1707 (according to her funeral sermon), gave 'an eminent instance of her charity' by:

> setting up and carrying on, for the last two summers successively, the ministry of the gospel, at her own charge, in a poor ignorant village, Sydenham, in Kent, not many miles from this city, and unto which many wealthy citizens with their families, in the summer, ordinarily resort (source 105: p. 394).

This summer mission has usually been considered, though without other evidence, as the origin of the Dissenters' meeting house at Sydenham. It certainly did exist in the 1740s.

Another benefit of the wells – possibly – was that they attracted medical men to the village. One of these was John Peter, who in 1681 published *A Treatise of Lewisham (but vulgarly miscall'd Dulwich) Wells in Kent*. He ends his little book in true professional style by declaring that:

> if any persons shall be pleased to confer with me about taking this water, if I am not at the wells, I shall be, God willing, ready at my house every day . . . to afford my best advice gratis; where also (if there shall be found occasion) they may be supplied (without any further trouble) with variety of medicinal preparations appropriated to the several distempers this water is to be used for (source 18: p. 10).

Dr Peter was one of those who had the good fortune to die (in 1684) just in time to avoid reading his epitaph.

Meanwhile developments were also taking place at the other end of the parish. The Lewisham frontages of Blackheath were still farmland when George Legge, later Lord Dartmouth, acquired the manor in 1673. He made a first step towards exploiting them in 1682, when he obtained permission to hold a fair on the Heath twice a year. In about 1688 the second Lord Dartmouth took the decisive step of annexing several acres on the western side of Blackheath, and laying out a street (Dartmouth Row) suitable for the fine suburban houses which were beginning to be in great demand among the wealthy Londoners. This was certainly an encroachment upon the Heath, but the Lewisham parish authorities had been squared by

An event closely linked with foundation of Blackheath Fai was the rebuilding of the Gre Man or Bowling Green Hous (an inn which had existed sin at least 1629) by 'Snape his Majesties farrier, a man full c projects', as John Evelyn call him. Snape's building of *c.* 1683, much altered and extended, is shown in this cru sketch of the early nineteenth century. The Green Man, whi stood at the corner of Dartmo Row and Blackheath Hill, wa rebuilt again in 1868, and fin demolished in 1971. The littl cupola with the weather vane the background on the right, belonged to the chapel built i Dartmouth Hill by Joshua Morton.

the offer of an annual sum in compensation for the loss of common rights.

Lord Dartmouth himself had a house in the Row, and over the decades it attracted other noble residents like the Earl of Lichfield, the Earl of Dumbarton and Viscount Falkland – mostly rather seedy Tories or Jacobites. But the majority of the tenants were from the City: aldermen, bank directors and leading lights of the great trading companies. These men added immensely to the wealth of the parish, though there was perhaps a tendency for the dwellers on the hill to hold themselves aloof from the village in the valley. This was emphasized in 1697 when Susannah Grahme, the first Lord Dartmouth's aunt, built a chapel in the Row and left funds to pay the vicar to hold a weekly service for this exclusive congregation.

The first to do so was George Stanhope, the most eminent of all the vicars of Lewisham. He was one of the great preachers of his day, and his translation of Thomas à Kempis, and his *Paraphrase and Comment on the Epistles and Gospels* were very popular books, reprinted well into the nineteenth century. He was chaplain to four monarchs and received regular advancement in the Church. Like a character in a Trollope novel he was only robbed of a bishopric by the untimely death of Queen Anne. Stanhope exercised some political influence as prolocutor (or chairman) of the lower house of convocation, at a time when the fate of governments could turn on a theological point.

George Stanhope (1660–1' who was Vicar of Lewisha from 1689 until his death, obtained the living as a rev for his services as tutor to first Earl of Dartmouth. He was also Vicar of Deptford from 1702, and Dean of Canterbury from 1704, but continued to live principal Lewisham.

Stanhope's acquaintance with the leading men of the day brought some famous visitors to Lewisham, and helped to make the village better known to the world. Jonathan Swift records that in July 1711 he and Francis Atterbury:

> passed the afternoon at Lewisham, at the Dean of Canterbury's; and there I saw Moll Stanhope, who is grown monstrously tall, but not so handsome as formerly. It is the first little rambling journey I have had this summer about London, and they are the agreeablest pastimes one can have, in a friend's coach, and to good company (source 102: pp. 208–9).

Mary Stanhope was the dean's daughter. In the next year her marriage to William, the son of Gilbert Burnet, Bishop of Salisbury, presumably meant that the Whig historian also visited the vicarage. The influence of Stanhope made Lewisham a place where a civilized man could live without feeling himself to be in Pontine exile.

This emergence from obscurity was assisted by the activities of the New Cross Turnpike Trust. When it was set up in 1717 the promoters claimed that the local roads had become so heavily used, especially for carting agricultural produce from rural Kent, and timber for the dockyards from Surrey and Sussex, that they had become almost useless for half of the year. The authority of the Trust to repair and maintain roads originally ran south only to St Mary's church. Two years later it was extended 'unto the first Mill-pond at South-end', now the Homebase Pool (source 84: p. 36), and in 1750 to the Lewisham boundaries with Bromley and Beckenham. The rapid improvement in road transport during this period was the essential foundation for the progress achieved in so many other fields after 1770.

Considering the width of his interests and the multifariousness of his duties, Stanhope was a conscientious vicar. His most solid memorial in Lewisham is the vicarage, which he rebuilt in 1692–3 at a cost of nearly £1,000. After the last sad century, in which all of its rivals have been destroyed, this house is now the oldest and best in central Lewisham. Stanhope also had ambitions to rebuild St Mary's church, which he described to Lord Dartmouth as in a very poor condition as the result of damp. Probably the parish was not yet quite rich or proud enough for such a major effort, and the old church was patched up for the time being.

Education was naturally of great interest to such a learned man as Stanhope. In his other parish of Deptford he built a charity school. In Lewisham, Abraham Colfe had made excellent provision for the schooling of boys, so in 1699 Stanhope turned his thoughts to the subject of female education. His foundation for thirty girls was originally supported by contributions from a body of aristocratic subscibers, and later by endowments left by Stanhope and his wife. It survived until 1833.

The inscription on Stanhope's tomb sums him up with smooth Augustan antithesis.

> [His] piety was real and rational, his charity great and universal, fruitful in acts of mercy and in all good works. His learning was elegant and comprehensive, his conversation polite and delicate, grave without preciseness, facetious without levity. The good Christian and solid divine, and the fine gentleman, in him were happily united . . . (source 62: p. 73).

It was during Stanhope's vicariate that industry first made a serious contribution to Lewisham's economy by taking advantage of the Ravensbourne. The cleansing properties of its water were vital in many industrial processes; and most of the important manufactures carried on in Lewisham exploited the river's power through the mills which had existed from Anglo-Saxon times. A probable third advantage of the Ravensbourne was its use as a means of transport. An act had been passed in the 1664–1665 session of Parliament empowering contractors to improve its navigation. It seems likely that this had some positive results as in the eighteenth century the Lewisham Bridge mill was used for the manufacture of luxury glassware, and it is incredible that a glassman would have moved his operation to Lewisham, if he had then been obliged to carry the goods to town by road. It seems almost certain that he could move them by boat from Lewisham Bridge to within a few hundred yards of his shop in Westminster.

The parish was not entirely without industries before the eighteenth century. The most important was carried on at the Armoury Mill, which stood on the boundary of Lewisham and Greenwich. From the fourteenth century until the Civil War this had been used for grinding the steel for the great royal armoury at Greenwich. The other significant early industries in Lewisham were connected with farming. Tanning was important in the seventeenth century, and perhaps earlier. There were tan yards on the site of the present hospital, and others further north, all on the west side of the High Street so as to give access to the Ravensbourne water. The activity in this field was such that in 1657 the manor court ordered that 'noe Inhabitant shall hange forth any skins or leather to dry in any of our foote paths or wayes to the annoyance of passengers' (source 90: SC 2/180/76). There were drying houses for animal skins at Lewisham Bridge, and the Riverdale mill was used for much of the eighteenth century, and into the nineteenth, for the manufacture of leather.

The Lewisham Nursery was founded in about 1736 by Henry Corbett, with its offices in an old High Street house called the Rookery, on the site now occupied by the United Reformed Church. Later in the century, under John Russell, it grew to be the largest nursery garden in the south of England, with 150 acres extending to Hither Green and Lee.

wisham Bridge Mill in the 30s or '40s, when it had urned to the grinding of n, after an interlude during ich it was used for the nufacture of cloth without aving, a process invented by seph Booth of Lewisham. e exterior of the building d probably not altered much ce the days of Thomas tts. It was replaced by a ch larger mill in the 1850s.

Early in the eighteenth century an important new industry was brought to the parish by Ephraim How, one of the great names in the history of English cutlery. He had founded his business at Chingford in Essex, but by 1709 had taken over the lower mill at Southend and used the power of the Ravensbourne to make 'those knife-blades so famous throughout England', which he sold at his shop on Saffron Hill, Holborn. How and his successors came to dominate the little village of Southend. Many of the houses were occupied by their employees, some of them skilled foreign craftsmen. By the Hows 'the art of cutlery was improved, and carry'd on to the greatest perfection', so that the upstarts from Sheffield took to imitating them by stamping the word NOW on their knife blades, in the hope of its being mistaken for HOW. After the closing of this business, the mill at Southend had other industrial uses – it was making mustard in 1810 – before returning to corn milling.

Reference has already been made to the use of Lewisham Bridge mill by a glass cutter. This was Thomas Betts, who lived and worked at Lewisham from 1756 until his death in 1765. The business was continued until the 1770s by Jonathan Collet, who married Betts' widow. It is interesting that shortly before his departure from Lewisham Collet was in correspondence with Matthew Boulton about the potential of steam power. It was the rise of steam that ended Lewisham's chief period of industrial activity.

Despite the great improvements taking place in the parish during Stanhope's days, Lewisham was still a village of contrasts. While the vicar sat in his study translating Epictetus and Marcus Aurelius, probate inventories reveal that one of the most valuable possessions of many of his neighbours was not the *Manual* or the *Golden Thoughts* – but dung.

One means by which the small farmers of Lewisham supplemented their uncertain incomes was baby farming, a major local industry throughout the eighteenth century, to judge from the numbers of nurse children who were buried each year. The regularity with which funerals proceeded from some houses leads to the suspicion that 'mortality guaranteed' was the claim with which their services were recommended, and it is likely that the graveyard of St Mary's concealed many a social indiscretion. Some of the nurse children were foundlings. The most popular place of deposit for these unfortunate infants was Blackheath, and the parish officials would respond as in this 1706 baptism: 'John Heath, so called because found at Blackheath at the boulding green house.' In 1819 another foundling was named Edward Heath.

In 1745 the parish was provided with a solid reminder of the penalties of failure in life. That, almost certainly, was the year in

This print, produced in 1841 mark the opening of John Thackeray's almshouses, als gives an excellent idea of the High Street stream. The mos interesting feature of the picture, though, is the buildi on the left, which in 1841 wa serving as the first Lewishan police station, but before 18 had almost certainly been th original parish workhouse.

which the first Lewisham workhouse was opened, on a site said to have been at the north end of Rushey Green, opposite George Lane. But the majority of relief was still paid to poor people living in their own homes. Many of these 'pentioners' received sums ranging from 1s. 5s. a week, which could be added to by carrying out parish chores like cleaning the workhouse, nursing orphans, sitting up with the sick, and stripping and laying out corpses. It is striking how detailed and personal and apparently humane was the attention of the overseers of the poor to their duties. Some of these supplementary payments from the 1760s have a strangely modern sound, except in the prices: 'To a Nurse for Goldsmith's wife a week, 3 shillings.' 'To the Widow Hall for Shoes for her Boy, 2s 3d.' 'To Mending Shoes for the Poor, 2s 4d.' 'To Binding Burgis Boy, 10s 6d' (an apprenticeship). 'To a Gown and Stays for Sarah Painter, 6s 9d.' 'To William Stevens his Familly having the Small Pox, 2s 6d.' 'To Mrs Walker for the Burial of her husband, etc., 10s.' 'To Wards Girl for Clothes to go to a Service, 10s 6d' (taking work as a servant). 'To John Harris for Widow Stevens's Lodging, 4s 6d.' 'To Judith Purnel to fetch her hat and Cloak out of Pawn, 2s 3d.' 'To a Shift, apron, and Cap for Applebys Girl to go into ye Hospital, 3s 6d.'

The overseers were constantly taking or sending patients to St Thomas's Hospital, and sometimes to Guy's, and expended large sums on transport, on medical bills, and in fees, tips and Christmas boxes for the beadles and other servants. Sometimes they would have to make several journeys if there was no bed available or if 'the Surgeons said it was to[o] hot Weather to do anything'.

Occasionally the overseers even administered a form of legal aid, most often in matters involving child maintenance, but also in this strange case from 1764:

> Attending a whole day on the justice to find out the person that gave the Child the foul Disease, 6s 8d. – Paid the Witnisses that Attended the justice to Clear the Man whom the Child charged with giving her the Foul Disease, 18s 6d (source 67: A59/37).

The regime in the workhouse itself may not have been too draconian, to judge from the money distributed to the inmates on the occasions of the christening of foundlings, and from the varied diet that is indicated by the foodstuffs bought by the overseers – unless, as in *Oliver Twist*, it was all intended for their own consumption. The most remarkable bargain they ever secured was 'to 6 pounds of Reasons, 2 shillings'.

Like nearly all parish officers the farmers and merchants who ran Lewisham's affairs were keen to minimize the number of paupers by preventing newcomers from settling in the village unless they were of solid means. Nevertheless the population was becoming more varied in the eighteenth century, with French cutlers at Southend and Bohemian glass scallopers at Lewisham Bridge. Black immigration into Lewisham is generally thought of as a phenomenon of the second half of the twentieth century, but in fact it probably began in the seventeenth, and was quite common in the eighteenth. Most, if not all, of the black inhabitants were brought to Lewisham as servants by the East and West Indian merchants and sea captains who settled there, as these extracts will show: in 1704, 'a black boy from Mr Richard Symes, caled Johnno'; 1717, 'Charles Nevis, a black moor, adult' and 'Anne, a black Moor, adult'; 1732, 'Mary, an adult negro from Madam Frere'; 1742, 'William, son of a Negro, from Mr Frere'; 1746, John Leeds, a Black, of MrKirk Patrick at Sydenham, aged about 19 years'; 1750, 'James Purcell, a black servant to Mr Purcell, at Mr Boydes at Lewisham, aged about 32 years'; 1767, 'to the Surgeon Opening the Negro Boy at Capt. Feattus's, £2 2s', and 'to the Jury on the Negro Boy, 10s' (a post mortem and inquest); 1776, 'William Taylor, a negro, found drowned near Rush Green'. Early in the nineteenth century 'Francis Edwards (the black boy)' and 'Richard Pemberton (the black)' received money from the parish charities. The most dramatic evidence comes from this advertisement of 1770:

> Run away on Wednesday, the 28th. ult., and stole money and goods from his master, John Lamb, Esq., an indentured black servant man about twenty-four years of age named William, of a brown or tawney complexion; had on when he went off, a parson's grey coat, blue breeches, white Bath flannel waistcoat, yellow gilt shoe buckles, and a beaver hat with a white lining.

> Whoever apprehends him and brings him to his master at the Rookery House in Lewisham, Kent, shall have ten guineas reward and ten more on conviction in court of any persons harbouring or concealing him either on board ship or on shore.
>
> N.B. He is also the property of his master, and has a burnt mark L.E., on one of his shoulders (source 41: pp. 136–7).

The variety of life was further added to by the excise officers deployed in Lewisham to combat smuggling, and by the large numbers of troops billeted at the local pubs. There were enough throughout the eighteenth century, and into the nineteenth, for the Black Bull to have a bar named 'the soldiers' room'. They helped, no doubt, to make Lewisham a rather violent place, particularly in the 1730s, when a surprising number of people (including an excise officer) were shot dead in the parish. Blackheath continued to be a notorious haunt of highwaymen, and in 1753 the respectable inhabitants of the area formed the first of their many associations for the prevention of crime. Despite this, the lurking highwayman probably had less to fear from the feeble police arrangements of the time than from the stray projectiles of another menace that then began to haunt the Heath, for it was in about 1750 that the Blackheath Golf Club seems to have been first established.

Fear of crime and social unrest may help to explain the comparatively friendly reception given to John Wesley and George Whitefield in Lewisham. When Wesley preached to between twelve and fourteen thousand people on Blackheath in 1739 (in a scene reminiscent of Bingo Little's memorable philippic at Speakers' Corner), he writes that 'I was greatly moved with compassion for the rich that were there, to whom I made a particular application. Some of them seemed to attend, while others drove away their coaches from so uncouth a preacher' (source 109: p. 86).

This preaching on Blackheath led to the old mound in the centre – possibly the grave of the Cornish rebels, and in the seventeenth century certainly the launching site for experimental mortars – receiving its permanent name of Whitefield's Mount. Whitefield and the two Wesley brothers were close friends of Jane Sparrow, a widow who lived at the Limes, one of the largest houses in the High Street. John Wesley in particular made use of the Limes as a country retreat and did a good deal of his writing there. Mrs Sparrow died in 1748, but that did not interrupt Wesley's visits, because the house was soon acquired by the banker Ebenezer Blackwell, who was the Methodist leader's financial advisor. Blackwell (who married the vicar's niece as his second wife) was one of the most influential members of the congregation at St Mary's church, which may be why Wesley was invited to preach there. Another reason is perhaps that he was favoured by the lord of the manor. The earls of Dartmouth were noted, often to the point of ridicule, for their piety and their support for evangelical causes. The Wesleys continued to be familiar figures in Lewisham until the death of Blackwell in 1782, when John Wesley noted in his diary:

> My brother and I paid our last visit to Lewisham, and spent a few pensive hours with the relict of our good friend, Mr Blackwell. We took one more walk round the garden and meadow, which he took so much pains to improve. Upwards of forty years this has been my place of retirement, when I could spare two or three days from London (source 109: p. 782).

Although the first seventy years of the eighteenth century did not produce much change in the pattern of settlement in Lewisham, these were decades of architectural progress, during which the ramshackle timber cottages that had dominated the village from its infancy began to be challenged for supremacy by smart new brick-built houses. Even in that medium the style was changing so rapidly that in 1745 William Lowth, the vicar, could describe Perceval House (in 1700, as it is today, one of the show pieces of Lewisham) in these disparaging terms:

> At the time when Mr Symes had made the Improvements to that house, as it was then very elegant & extreamly in the Fashion, the Rent of £100 was very moderate, [but] ye Manner, & what they call the Taste for Buildings and Country Houses is so entirely different from what it was at that time, that the Fashion of that House will be now despis'd, and a larger & another sort of Out-lett will be desir'd, than that house has. It should

-ceval House, built in 1689 Sir Martin Beckman, is the -t preserved of the original -rtmouth Row houses, -ugh it is now divided, with -f being called Spencer -use. The assassinated prime -nister had no connection -h the mansion, but his -sman Lord Perceval did live -re from 1813 to 1818. This -tch was executed in 1841, -en Miss Sapientia Stone ran fashionable boarding -ool at Perceval House.

likewise be consider'd that at the end of 17 years more the House will be pretty old (source 67: PT 80/426/24).

Timber was still widely used, especially for the public houses and farms built in this period, like the Greyhound at Sydenham in about 1720, the Plough (originally the Sun) in 1722, the old George near the church in 1732, the Two Brewers in about 1745, and the farm that is now Elmwood (the Catford Conservative Club) in 1736. For private houses, though, brick had become the favourite material. The rich merchants who built them had, by 1770, become the leaders of Lewisham, and they lost no time in reshaping the parish to suit their own tastes and interests. Although this generation of City men had mostly changed the outward form of their religion, they remained the true heirs of the puritans in their deep distrust of the pleasures of the people.

During the spring and summer Westwood Common had become the venue for an informal fair, widely patronized by servants and apprentices. It was nominally for the sale of birds and birds' nests, but really for the enjoyment of drinking, romping, and promiscuous fun and games in the countryside. By 1766 this assembly had caused such alarm to the 'principal inhabitants of Lewisham and Sydenham . . . and the villages adjacent' that they mounted an impressive and successful petition to the Quarter Sessions at Maidstone to have it suppressed. Their chief complaint was that these 'meetings or Assemblys consist of several Hundreds of the most dissolute and profligate Persons of both Sexes from all Parts of London and its Environs' and that they contributed 'to the ruin of many Apprentices and other young Persons who are induced to attend these Meetings to the great Neglect of their Masters and Familys and the Encouragement of Vice and Immorality' (source 59).

In 1772 Lord Dartmouth acted to curtail the Blackheath fair which his predecessor had established ninety years before. It had been intended principally for the sale of cattle, but Evelyn remarked after the very first in 1683 that 'there appeared nothing but an innumerable assemblie of drinking people from London, Pedlers, etc.: & I suppose it too neere London to be of any greate use for the Country' (source 36: IV 311). It had continued to be a highly popular entertainment, with freak shows and the like, but these regular gatherings of the common people on the common were alarming to Lord Dartmouth's wealthy tenants. He now restricted the fair to two days a year and decreed that only cattle might be sold. A further blow had been struck for respectability in its never ending battle with fun.

CHAPTER FOUR

Opulent Merchants (1770–1840)

is wonderfully detailed cture of Catford Bridge – the l with the toy horse, the vers in the arbour – was inted in about 1830, by an known artist. The view is uth westwards towards vensbourne Park, the lodge which can be glimpsed on extreme right. Catford idge Mill, on the left, was t one of the eleven ntioned in Domesday Book. was only founded in about 00.

Lewisham now entered the period of its greatest prosperity and beauty. The new masters of the village cared far more about its appearance and amenities than their farming predecessors, and they had the money to change things that displeased them. What they were intent on creating was the suburban idyll at its most complete – the countryside tamed but still romantic. Their villas usually had gardens large enough to give a pleasing illusion of wildness. At Southend, for example, the Forster family, the chief landowners in the parish, had a private park of 120 acres.

Descriptions of Lewisham at this period show that it commanded greater respect from strangers, and inspired the residents with pride and boastfulness. In 1776 Edward Hasted wrote that:

> The village of Lewisham consists of one street, of more than a mile in length, in which are numbers of neat and handsome houses, inhabited by opulent merchants and traders of the city of London, the vicinity of which makes this place a most agreeable and convenient recess for them . . . . There are several hamlets in this parish, which are interspersed with neat and elegant houses, filled with opulent inhabitants; among which Southend, Pery-street, and Sydenham, are the most considerable (source 48: I 74–5).

In 1785 a chauvinistic local told Sylvanus Urban that:

> It is very remarkable that the parish of Lewisham pays more duty to government for carriages than the two neighbouring parishes of Greenwich and Deptford. So much is that village improved, which formerly was stigmatized by the appellation of 'long, lazy, lousy Lewisham'; but now is, with propriety, called 'lovely, lively, loyal Lewisham' (source 4).

During the last three decades of the eighteenth century and the first three of the nineteenth the pictorial evidence confirms that the parish was being rapidly improved. In the years around 1770 Carrington Bowles, an eminent London print seller, published a series of Lewisham views that show a still quite primitive scene – rutted and muddy roads, unkempt ponds and greens, tumbledown wooden houses. By the 1830s the paintings and prints feature elegant stucco villas, well-maintained roads, and carefully tended

An ambitious public work carried out by the Lewisham vestry was the building of a brick bridge at Ladywell in 1830. There had previously been only the wooden footbridge shown here in James Bourne's watercolour *c.* 1810. Wheeled traffic had splash through the river. St Mary's appears on the right. The block just left of centre was the slum terrace called Brockley Place, which clung the garden wall of Lewisham House.

lawns and streams and ornamental waters. Lewisham and Lee bridges were rebuilt in a style suitable to the greater quality of the roads, and this also encouraged the growth of the excellent coach services that now took many City men to work. These coaches became important local institutions, competing with the parish church and the great inns as marts for gossip and scandal.

The most conspicuous public work undertaken during this great period of improvement was the rebuilding of St Mary's between 1774 and 1777. The medieval church, small, low, and damp, had long been inadequate to the needs of the growing parish, but until this time the task of replacing it had appeared too daunting. The composition of the committee that oversaw the work was significant. At first it was the ordinary local officeholders, several of them still farmers, who dominated. For the decisive meetings at which it was decided to rebuild rather than repair, the big guns, Lords Dartmouth and Falkland, were brought up, but once detailed matters of design and finance came into question it was the City men – Thomas Hicks, Alderman Samuel Turner, and the banker Ebenezer Blackwell – who took control. In the end Blackwell advanced the entire sum needed for the building work – at four per cent interest.

The committee took the bold step of appointing George Gibson as architect, even though they were in contact with the considerably more eminent George Dance the younger. Gibson had recently given up his practice in London and moved to Deptford, where he dramatically signalled his arrival by building, for his own use, the remarkable villa called Stone House. This magnificent but distinctly eccentric creation, just completed in 1773, was popularly known as Comical House. The solid citizens on the St Mary's committee may have been more impressed by the fact that the great plutocrat John Julius Angerstein had chosen Gibson to design his villa, Woodlands, near Blackheath.

The new St Mary's was first used for worship in 1777. The church was partly financed from the rental of the pews, and competition for the best of these was to be an important social activity throughout Lewisham's fashionable period. Parishioners could also display their wealth by erecting great monuments in this as yet uncluttered building. Some superb examples of the 1780s and '90s are to be found in St Mary's, sculpted by the leading artists of the day (Banks, for example, and Flaxman), and one with verses by the fashionable poet William Hayley. With the retreat of the wealthy in the twentieth century these monuments are now probably the finest works of art existing in Lewisham.

Education responded to the changes in the parish. Colfe's English School for boys and Stanhope's school for girls continued as before, but Colfe's grammar school had become unrecognizable. It was a

The new St Mary's, seen here in 1790, was described in 178[illegible] as being 'distinguished for its beautiful neatness and simplicity'. It received scant justice from the dogmatic Victorians ('ugly, and built without taste' is a typical comment from 1878), but is now properly appreciated once more. Gibson pleased the antiquarians by retaining the old tower, merely raising and ornamenting it to harmonize with his design.

characteristic of the eighteenth century for corporations to decay while individual initiative flourished. The Leathersellers' Company had exercised less and less control, and allowed the headmasters to neglect Colfe's plans for the benefit of 'ordinary people', while building up (for their own profit) the private boarding aspect of the school. Colfe's name was almost forgotten, and the establishment was usually called Mr Norton's, or Mr Williams's School, after the headmaster of the day.

The limited boarding accommodation at the grammar school did not suffice for long. In 1785 a new trend was announced in a long and pompous advertisement from Messrs Marr, late of Upper Clapton, who were, they said, 'averse from the common practice of advertising'. They had bought Lewisham House, the largest and best mansion in the High Street, and converted it for use as an exclusive private academy, where only French was 'permitted to be spoken in the school or family' (source 4).

Lewisham School, as it came to be called, did not survive the deaths of its founders, but its example was followed over the next century by countless other private academies, especially in Blackheath, Sydenham and Forest Hill. They varied a good deal in quality – David Copperfield's Salem House is a portrait of a bad one at Blackheath – but by and large maintained a good reputation. Most, like the one in Eliot Place attended by Benjamin Disraeli, were for boys, but Blackheath had some outstanding private schools for girls as well. The learned Margaret Bryan started one in South Row in 1799, and from the 1830s there were two notable schools in Dartmouth Row: a progressive establishment, kept by the aunts of Robert Browning, and a fashionable one, presided over by a lady with the wonderfully (perhaps too wonderfully) appropriate name of Sapientia Stone.

These schools attracted pupils from far afield, often from the colonies, but they also had a growing potential market much closer at hand, for this was a period when the number of good quality houses in and around Lewisham was increasing apace. In the south of the parish the most important new development was the original Forest Hill (now Honor Oak Road), which was laid out in the 1780s on an ambitious scale reminiscent of Dartmouth Row a century earlier. At the same time Sydenham was growing rapidly, and Hither Green, previously a small hamlet of farms and cottages, began its career as an exclusive residential area.

Overshadowing all of these developments was the remarkable growth of Blackheath during the 1790s. The nucleus of the village had existed early in the century, as had the Hare and Billet, and some neighbouring cottages; and Grotes Place and Lloyds Place were added in the 1760s and '70s. Apart from these, the southern edge of the Heath was occupied in 1790 by the park of Wricklemarsh House to the east of the village, and by Lord Eliot's farmland to the west. Lord Eliot (whose son became the first Earl of St Germans in 1815) decided early in the decade that this valuable frontage was ripe for exploitation. By 1795 the fine group known as Eliot Place had begun to appear, and was joined by other desirable residences further west, including one house (The Knoll) probably designed by George Gibson, the architect of St Mary's. Almost simultaneously John Cator of Beckenham, who had bought Wricklemarsh in 1783, and had begun to demolish the palatial house in 1787, also decided to develop the Heath frontage of his estate. Michael Searles designed the Paragon and South Row, including the striking villa called Colonnade House, but it is not known whether he was responsible for Montpelier Row. At the same time the village was assuming something like its modern shape, and numbers of houses were being built in Blackheath Hill. During the decade from 1795 to 1805 the population of the Lewisham part of Blackheath certainly doubled, and may have trebled.

The newcomers were people of fashion and wealth, or at least – like the Paragon confidence trickster Miss Elizabeth Robertson – those able to assume a veneer of such solid qualities. Blackheath had long attracted its share of aristocratic residents. Now royalty began to favour it, with the retirement of Caroline, Princess of Wales, to Montagu House on her separation from the prince in 1799. George III dutifully visited his vulgar daughter-in-law from time to time, and came with greater pleasure when his sister, the Duchess of Brunswick, mother of Caroline, also took refuge at Blackheath (in Chesterfield House) in 1807. Montagu House adjoined Greenwich Park, but it had only a small garden there, and Caroline spent much time at its detached summer-house on the Lewisham side of the Heath. This was the Pagoda, which had been built by the fourth Earl of Cardigan, probably in 1767. Caroline used it for the nursery school with which she tried to fill her empty life. Her extreme – some said maternal – attachment to a boy named William Austin was one of the many scandals on which the Prince of Wales later attempted to ground a divorce. The chief scandalmongers were Sir John and Lady Douglas of no. 8 Montpelier Row, and it is interesting to note that when their daughter was baptized at St Mary's in 1802 the Princess of Wales had been one of the sponsors.

The prosperity indicated by all these luxury developments could only breed discontent. Symbolic of this was the appearance in the parish of the arch-rebel John Wilkes, as the guest of Sir Benjamin Hammet. Hammet had bought Grove House, one of the most important properties in Lewisham High Street, and in 1786 the newspapers recorded a curious meeting there of a seditious fraternity of self-dubbed 'knights':

> Alderman Sir Benjamin Hammet gives a grand dinner on Michaelmas-day next, at his house at Lewisham, to Sir John Wilkes, Sir Brook Watson and Lady Watson, Doctor Prettyman, Major Scott, Mr and Mrs Hastings, and all the new Knights Burgesses of the Blade in Westminster. Messrs Brooker, Corbet, and Holt, of Lewisham, are appointed stewards, and will on the Monday following receive the honor of knighthood. Lady Hammet gives a grand rout in the evening to the ladies of Greenwich and Blackheath (source 4).

Streete House, as drawn by Charles Bullard in 1833. It wa[s] named after Humphrey Stree[t] who gave the property to the parish in 1626, though the house was evidently rebuilt i[n] the eighteenth century. After Joshua Morton's departure it was occupied by a successio[n] of doctors, including the kee[n] toxophilite Methusalem Davies. Streete House survives, much altered, as the Hire Shop.

Characteristically, most of the quarrels that shook Lewisham during its prosperous period were connected with religion. The most entertaining was the dispute between the elderly vicar William Lowth and his curate, Joshua Morton. Like most such affairs it was probably at root the result of incompatibility of temperament, but the immediate cause of hostilities was offered by the Dartmouth Chapel. Morton had conducted the services at Blackheath since his arrival in the parish in 1778, but Lowth had continued to pocket the stipend. In the revolutionary year of 1789 Morton decided to claim payment for his years of work at the chapel, and was promptly sacked. He lived at Streete House in Lewisham, but for some time had been running a school at the vicarage. Now he transferred it to the corner of Dartmouth Row and Grove, where he had 'a large brass Plate fixt to his door, and engraved upon it The Revd Mr Morton's Private Seminary for a select number of Young Gentlemen'; and he began to build a chapel in

Dartmouth Hill as a rival to the one in Dartmouth Row. The affair divided the parish, with Morton's body of supporters including Wilkes's friend Sir Benjamin Hammet. Lord Dartmouth's steward, a strong anti-Mortonite, sent his master this account of local gossip:

> I went to Town last monday in the Lewisham Stage with Mr St Barbe and he speaking of Mr Morton's School . . . said he always lookt on Morton as an impertinant fellow, meddling with every bodys business; a Greenwich Gentleman said he was a damned fool, and a woman threw in her mite, she said he was a Tyrant in his Family, that I have heard often and called a Bashaw. . . . He I hear denies part of his impertinance to Mr Lowth, people says he is very apt to tell fibs; these are heavy charges to give a Minister, very opposite to meekness and humility (source 67: PT 80/426/42).

The most prominent aspect of the growth of Lewisham in the late eighteenth century was the huge increase in luxury housing, but where the rich go the poor are sure to follow if they possibly can. The rich, indeed, require a manageable number of them to satisfy their many needs, reputable and otherwise. There had been no established working class areas in the parish, the small houses being scattered all around the large ones in traditional rural chaos. Now a few new settlements of the poor began to emerge where the wide borders of certain roads offered sites for cottages. The most important of these was the wasteland village of Ladywell, which rose rapidly from next to nothing in the 1780s, almost entirely as a result of this process of piecemeal enclosure. Lord Dartmouth was happy to sanction it because, at the expiration of the original leases, the freeholds passed to him. In 1789 his steward was able to report that 'the parish of Lewisham is greatly increased with some of the most useful sort, which are labouring people'. Did the earl take a different view of their usefulness when he began to receive an annual demand for his subscription to the Lewisham school of industry? Probably not, as he was a pious man, and charitable in small things, though on the great question of the Lewisham enclosure his sympathies were entirely with his own class.

The school of industry was established in about 1795 on the site later occupied by the new workhouse, and now by the southern range of the hospital. It was intended to train boys and girls (who might otherwise have run wild and become a danger to the rich) for useful employment. As the nineteenth century advanced, a horrible traffic in pauper children emerged. Manufacturers from Lancashire and Yorkshire began to make regular visits to acquire Lewisham children as apprentices, and transport them north into something not widely different from slavery. Yet at the same time, Robert Arnold of the Lewisham Silk Mills was in the habit of importing his apprentices from the inner London parishes. Presumably the masters did not want their regimes overlooked by any possible friends of the children.

Lewisham's industry was in gradual decline as one by one the water mills returned to the grinding of corn, but some new employers did appear. Lime burning and brickmaking had been carried on for many years in the Loampit Hill area. The arrival of the Lee brothers, John and Henry, in the 1790s, at a time when house building in Blackheath and Lewisham was rapidly increasing, marked a serious escalation in this activity.

A major new source of employment was opened in 1807 when the government decided to establish a small arms factory at the moribund Armoury Mills, with the intention of stimulating the gunmakers of Birmingham to greater efforts by this threatened competition. It was a mixed blessing. Many of the specialist workmen were imported from less civilized regions of the country and brought with them habits very noxious to the staid citizens of Lewisham. Not least among them was bull baiting:

> a Diversion so immediately injurious to the moral Feelings of the Inhabitants, threatening to endanger the Lives, not only of the Parties engaged, but of the unguarded Passenger, and in its Consequences to disturb in various other Ways the general Peace of the Public (source 9: 3 October 1812).

The local magistrates, though (as they most untruthfully declared) 'far from wishing to interrupt the lower Classes of the Community in the Indulgence of any wholesome and innocent Diversions', took steps in 1812 to ban the sport.

This was not the end of the troubles caused to Lewisham by the

The Armoury Mills were sold by the Board of Ordnance, an[d] rapidly adapted to the very different purpose of convertin[g] raw silk into the finished form. This 1841 watercolour is the earliest known image of the Lewisham Silk Mills.

small arms factory, for with the coming of peace in 1815 more than half of the men were laid off, and in 1818 production stopped altogether. As a result the new Lewisham workhouse began to fill with gunsmiths, lock filers, and barrel forgers, who had little chance of finding similar employment in the district.

For the accommodation of the men at the Armoury Mills, in the brickfields, and in the service trades increasingly demanded by the wealthy, Lewisham's first large working class districts were built at the beginning of the nineteenth century. There were two of them, both characteristically replaced in our own time by the most up-to-date variety of high-rise slum. The first, partly in Greenwich, lay in the angle of Lewisham Road and Blackheath Hill. It was known as Loat's Pit because it was an area from which, over centuries, all the valuable materials had been dug by the brickmaker Lancelot Loat and his predecessors. This arid waste land was now useless for anything except the housing of the poor, and was quickly covered with a network of squalid streets, plus a pub for the gunmakers called the Ordnance Arms. The second working-class area lay to the south of Loampit Vale. Mill Lane, the approach road to Lewisham Bridge Mill, began to be lined with cottages from about 1790, and

t's Pit in 1925, painted by Vidnell Wilson, who had set his easel in Carthage Street, inally called Queen Street. turning to the right was wich Place, formerly Essex ce. This slum, a cause of e shame and alarm to the lthy residents of ckheath, was largely royed by Second World bombing, as was Holy ity Church in Blackheath , which looms in the kground.

the reputation of their tenants was such that the name Botany Bay became almost officially attached to this quarter. In 1800 it was the seat of a serious outbreak of smallpox. Between Botany Bay and the brickfields of the Lee brothers lay some market-garden ground belonging to a family named Fox. When they decided, in about 1800, to exploit it for housing they had little option, with such unwelcome neighbours on either side, but to build workers' cottages. The Fox's Fields development, comprising Elmira Street, Porson Street and Cross Street, was practically complete by 1810.

These were striking changes to the Lewisham landscape, but they did not announce a trend. Apart from some slums produced by the Lewisham enclosure, Loat's Pits and Fox's Fields were the only specifically working class areas in the parish until quite late in the nineteenth century, although there were numerous courts and alleyways off the High Street, Rushey Green and Blackheath village, in which small communities of workers were hidden from sight.

The population, which was probably about 2,700 in 1770, had risen to 4,007 in 1801, when there were 722 houses in the parish. By 1811 the total was 6,625 people in 1,105 houses, with nearly 100 more empty or being built. Of the 1,272 families only 214 were chiefly engaged in agriculture, 261 chiefly in trade, manufactures, or handicrafts, and 797 in neither. This indicates the extent to which Lewisham was already a commuting or retirement suburb, as does the remarkable sexual disparity of 2,923 males against 3,702 females. This excess of 800 women was largely made up of domestic servants, working in the homes of those who drew their incomes from outside the parish. It was to continue into the twentieth century, and was in sharp contrast to the position in industrial areas like Woolwich, where there were significantly more men than women.

The pauper population was not rising as a proportion of the whole, but it was certainly rising fast in absolute terms. The parish authorities responded in 1814 by obtaining a private Act of Parliament empowering them to replace the workhouse. The old building was abandoned and a new site purchased from Lord Dartmouth. It was a house – perhaps the old manor farm of Lewisham – then being used as a school of industry, and as a factory for employing the poor in making stockings. This was demolished and the new workhouse built in 1817. It survives as part of the hospital. Here was a first step in the harsher treatment of the poor, who were now far more likely to be taken into the workhouse and less likely to be relieved in their own homes. The final triumph of utilitarianism followed in 1836, when the Lewisham Union, a combination of seven parishes, established its headquarters here, and a grinding bureaucracy took charge of the whole melancholy business.

The workhouse was not quite the only resource for those struggling with poverty. Over the centuries a number of charitable citizens had left sums of money to the poor, and these were distributed annually in cash, or in kind. Lists of the recipients have survived and show a surprisingly even spread of hardship, with just as much money going to Blackheath and Sydenham as to Lewisham and Catford. One lady who was glad to receive 10s. every two years from Hatcliffe's Charity was Widow Larkin, whose poignant address was 'near Workhouse'.

A significant date in the history of Lewisham is 1810, the year in which the Enclosure Act was passed. This and the coming of the Crystal Palace were the two key events in the shaping of Sydenham and Forest Hill. That district had recently had its quiet growth disturbed by the slow digging of the Croydon Canal (opened in 1809) across a corner of the common. But the commercial failure of that venture meant that its significance was largely potential, as affording the basic route for the Croydon Railway in years to come. For the present it added to the amenities of the area – once the navvies had moved on – by the fishing, sailing, swimming and shooting that could be enjoyed on the canal and its reservoir. In other respects Sydenham's growth had been rather similar to Blackheath's. Fine detached houses and imposing terraces had begun to encircle the common, taking advantage of the wonderful undulating prospects it offered. As at Blackheath, the population included many wealthy merchants and the odd aristocrat, but there was also a distinctly Bohemian flavour, with a sprinkling of artists, actors and poets enjoying the most picturesque part of Lewisham.

)mas Campbell caricatured Daniel Maclise for *Fraser's gazine* in 1830. He did his t to carry on the tradition of nken Sydenham poets ablished by Dermody, but not always keep a good :k in the house, and would : his distinguished guests to Greyhound, from which he netimes had to be helped ne to bed.

The most picturesque of the poets was the feckless Irishman Thomas Dermody, who, when asked why he had lived such a vicious life, replied, 'because I like it'. He died in 1802 in a 'wretched hovel' in Perry Slough (now Perry Vale), while in hiding from his creditors. The most celebrated poet was Thomas Campbell, who lived in a house in Peak Hill, overlooking the common, from 1804 until 1820. For most of that time he was carrying on a thwarted love affair with the great heiress of the village, Mary Mayow – thwarted because of Campbell's unhappy marriage to a woman with nothing poetical about her except her name, which was Matilda. The Peak Hill house was visited by many of the great writers and artists of the day, including Scott, Byron, Moore, Crabbe, Mrs Siddons and Sir Thomas Lawrence.

Sydenham Common, like Blackheath, had been nibbled away by piecemeal enclosure for centuries. Coleson's Coppice in the north (the Honor Oak Road area) and Cooper's Wood in the south (Lawrie Park) had been enclosed in the seventeenth century or earlier, and throughout the eighteenth the earls of Dartmouth and their manor court were regularly authorizing small encroachments near

Sydenham Road and Westwood Hill. These provoked the odd riot and lawsuit, and in 1789 this Jacobin remonstrance to the earl from a Sydenham farmer named John Trehearn:

> I am Sory your Lordship should Ofer to Take Part of West Wood Common without the Consent of the Freholders Caled Coopers Wood . . . your Jury must Say as you Pleas or be Turnd of, I know it Sartin well by experance (source 67: PT 80/426/40).

Along the wide borders of Perry Vale, which formed practically an extension to the common, Lord Dartmouth forbad enclosures on the north side, where the bordering land belonged to him, but gladly allowed them on the south side, next to the land of Mayow Wynell Mayow, much to that gentleman's fury. Such nuisances continued until the great men were ready to make a final division of the common land.

The principal sponsors of the enclosure were 'George Earl of Dartmouth, the Right Honourable John Lord Eliot, Sir Francis Baring Baronet, Francis Motley Austen Esquire, John Forster Esquire, William Allen Esquire'. These six had one striking point in common: none of them lived at Sydenham, and the only one who owned land there was Lord Dartmouth, who owned land everywhere. The practice at enclosures was for the common land to be shared among the freeholders in proportion to the size of their estates, which meant that Lord Dartmouth, Forster, and the others would be the great winners, and the poor people (who used the common for grazing their animals and gathering fuel) the great losers. Opposition to the rather different enclosure attempt of the early seventeenth century had been led by the vicar, Abraham Colfe. In 1810 the vicar was conspicuous by his silence. This was Edward Legge, afterwards Bishop of Oxford and Warden of All Souls, who by a coincidence very far from strange, was the Earl of Dartmouth's brother. It is not clear whether the Legges, who had a reputation for piety and dullness, followed the common aristocratic practice of sending the fool of the family into the Church, but Edward Legge was certainly incautious enough to invite the witty Canning and Frere to his inaugural sermon as bishop:

> 'Well,' said he to Canning, 'how did you like it?' 'Why, I thought it rather – short.' 'Oh, yes, I am aware that it was short; but I was afraid of being tedious.' 'You *were* tedious' (source 95: p. 115).

The Enclosure Act did not pass entirely without opposition. All would no doubt have gone quite smoothly but for Lord Dartmouth's determination that Sydenham Common and all the smaller pieces of waste ground (Rushey Green, Hither Green, Bell Green, etc.) should be enclosed, but that Blackheath, where *he* lived, should be exempt. Posterity is duly grateful for the obstinacy with which the earl maintained his point, but at the time it was greeted with outrage in Sydenham, which was apt to be resentful in any case of its government by a Lewisham vestry in which Sydenham men played little part.

The Sydenhamites, as those were called who opposed the enclosure unless it should include Blackheath, were led by Joseph Marryat, MP for Horsham, the father of Captain Marryat the novelist. The family, who lived at Malvern House in Sydenham Road, were all of a passionate nature, and Joseph's anger at the enclosure plan was doubtless sharpened by the fact that he occupied his large estate only as a leaseholder, which meant that he stood to gain little or nothing by the Act. For a time the prospects for either the enclosure or Blackheath looked distinctly bleak, but when Sir Francis Baring was won over, Lord Dartmouth's agent wrote confidently (and revealingly):

> I am extremely glad to find Sir Francis Baring is so steadily inclined to co-inside with Lords Dartmouth and Eliot in the Inclosure of Sydenham Common and the half year Lands, and of keeping Blackheath open. I have no doubt but by perseverance we shall carry our object, for though there are many Persons against the measure their property is inconsiderable (source 67: A 62/6/134).

The bill eventually passed its second reading by one vote, after two opponents accidentally missed the division.

The enclosure brought great physical changes to many other parts of the parish. In Lewisham village itself it meant the building over of Plough Green, at the northern corner of the High Street and Loampit Vale (the site of an annual fair), and of Watch House Green. The latter is now covered by the banks and shops between the High Street and Lewis Grove. This was the real village green, a camping ground for the yeomanry, and a preaching site for itinerant Methodists. Here stood the stocks, the cage and the whipping post.

Rushey Green and Bell Green were divided into small allotments for minor freeholders, which meant that they were built over in a disorganized way as areas of small cottages and alleyways, occupied by the poor. This decisively changed the destiny of those two districts, which had previously been quite smart, with detached houses scattered around the greens. At Catford one of these – Elmwood – still survives. Its alignment to the modern road pattern would be thoroughly mysterious without this clue.

Sydenham and Forest Hill were changed utterly by the enclosure. About a third of the district now called by those names was built on the common in the next sixty years. The commissioners followed the inegalitarian rule of placing the small allotments together in the lower lying parts, and the larger ones on the valuable high ground.

These small plots were not viable for agricultural use, so most of them were built on quite rapidly. The result was a dense development of cottages – often wooden – in the streets now called Kirkdale, Wells Park Road, Dartmouth Road and Perry Vale, and in the numerous culs-de-sac branching from them. These culs-de-sac became a feature of the district as the various new owners pursued their individual and uncoordinated building schemes.

On the higher ground towards Sydenham Hill a certain number of large houses appeared in the 1820s and '30s, but progress was hampered by the lack of water. This forced on builders the expensive necessity of sinking a deep well for each house, and as a result many landowners were happy to sell or lease their allotments to John Forster of Southend, Lewisham's Midas. He thus built up a farm of some 125 acres in and around Westwood Hill, which was to prove of incalculable value when the Crystal Palace came to Sydenham.

In other parts of the parish detached villas continued to appear on surrendered farmland. Water supply was not a problem in the village itself: the High Street stream was an immemorial source and piped water became available soon after 1809, when the proprietors of the Kent Waterworks at Deptford were empowered to extend their operations to Lewisham. The Strawberry Hill Gothic villa known as the Priory was, like Strawberry Hill, a transformed farmhouse. It is likely that the transformation occurred during the period (1793–1813) when it was occupied by Charles Churchill, the brother-in-law of Horace Walpole, who created Strawberry Hill. In 1816 the attractions of the Priory included 'a beautiful trout stream, forming a handsome sheet of water' (source 4). Peacocks stalked the lawns of several villas, including Rosenthal (the home of the macassar oil king Alexander Rowland) and Catford House.

Bromley Hill, the largest mansion in Lewisham, was being created during this period by Charles Long, Lord Farnborough (1761–1838). He bought the house in about 1795 and spent the next forty years enlarging and embellishing it. Long was a close friend of William Pitt, and the prime minister was a frequent visitor to Bromley Hill, which he liked to use for important political meetings. The house survives as the Bromley Court Hotel.

The most striking development of the 1820s was Ravensbourne Park, a luxury estate in the tradition of Dartmouth Row and the original Forest Hill. It included a few large houses (long since demolished) and a number of handsome semi-detached pairs, some of which survive. A notable feature of Ravensbourne Park was the covenant preserving a generous proportion of open land among the houses. The crescent surrounds one of these reserved meadows.

A rich and leisured population needed entertainment. Hunting was

posite: Mr Skinner's House' uly 1805, by an artist who ferred to remain nymous. Although George nner lived in Lewisham gh Street (at the corner of mont Hill), his house was Lee, for the Quaggy River, npsed on the left, was the ish boundary. The point of w is roughly from the site he clock tower, and on the nt is the north end of Watch use Green, where the lland and Barclays banks v stand. So this tranquil t is today the frenzied tre of Lewisham.

ow: The stocks and ipping-post on Watch use Green. As late as 1804 a respondent of John Dunkin 'a man and woman ipped at the whipping post ewisham. I believe they been robbing gardens.' urce 34: I 218) available in and around Sydenham, where the Old Surrey – Mr Jorrocks's hunt – used to meet at the Greyhound, until the enclosure forced it farther into the country. Even in the 1830s the Fox and Hounds in Kirkdale was a rendezvous for the West Kent Hounds. Sporting grocers of the Jorrocks type were welcome in the parish, but this toleration did not extend to every case. In 1786 it came to the attention of the magistrates that:

> there is a Pack of Hounds kept by a man at Sydenham, who is nothing more than a day labourer, and is frequently out, and a parcel of Idle fellows attending the Hunt, who . . . ought to be imploying themselves in the maintainance of their familys (source 67: PT 80/426/34).

This scratch hunt, which had its headquarters at the Dog Kennel Houses, in the modern Silverdale area, was rapidly suppressed.

Archery was much in vogue in the 1780s and '90s, at Ladywell, where the St George's Bowmen met under the captaincy of Methusalem Davies, the village doctor, and on Blackheath. The Heath was also used as a golf course, the oldest outside Scotland. Cricket was popular on the Heath from the eighteenth century, and early in the nineteenth at Sydenham, where there was a pitch behind the Golden Lion, and another in the private grounds of the Lawrie family near Westwood Hill. Bowls and skittles were played in the gardens of public houses. At the Roebuck in Lewisham High Street patrons could enjoy cricket, shooting, swimming, and the 'new and interesting game of Hindoo or Turf Billiards, an easy and pleasant exercise, combined with science and skill' (source 45: 29 March 1834).

The local magistrates were happy to countenance these sports, and

'Mr Staley's House near Ravensbourne Park', seen h in February 1836, was one the large detached propertie on that estate. James Staley had the house built in about 1830, and was probably the first occupant, but by 1837 had let it to an Irish East Indian merchant named Bro Roberts. Bournville Road ha taken the place of this hous which was demolished in th 1890s.

Catford House in Catford H painted by the young John Gilbert (later Sir John) in about 1835. In 1838 it was described as 'a small but ve elegant house . . . The grou have been laid out with gre taste, at considerable expen The interior . . . is decorate with paintings by Correggi Rembrandt, Cranius, Domenichino, Claude, Teni Rubens, and Salvator Rosa' (source 46: p. 24). Catford House was demolished in 1895.

the betting that accompanied them, but it was quite another matter when it came to pedestrianism. The walking of long distances for wagers was common on Blackheath in the eighteenth century and the first half of the nineteenth. These events alarmed the authorities by drawing large and thirsty crowds of spectators, with the inevitable accompaniment of rival attractions and sideshows. When, in 1815, George Wilson undertook to walk a thousand miles in as many hours, and was arrested when well on the way to accomplishing the feat, the justices earned widespread ridicule for their 'unwarrantable warrant against walking'.

Intellectual pleasures were in shorter supply than the physical, no doubt because in less demand, though the 1830s was a period when the *Kentish Mercury* found room for translations from Horace. The wealthy could see such plays as they desired in London. Locally, the thespian art was only upheld by the disreputable theatres at Deptford and Greenwich, which led a precarious existence under the watchful eye of the local bench. There was music-making of a sort in public

orge Wilson arraigned fore the Blackheath Bench the Mitre Tavern, eenwich. The caricaturist's ost serious allegation, ntained in the scales of tice, is that the magistrates ervened because they had t heavily against Wilson's ccess. The chairman at this eting was James Rice lliams of Lee. Abraham nstable, the Lewisham ewer, was also present, but idently declined to act. stead he had a violent gument with Williams, and s himself threatened with prisonment.

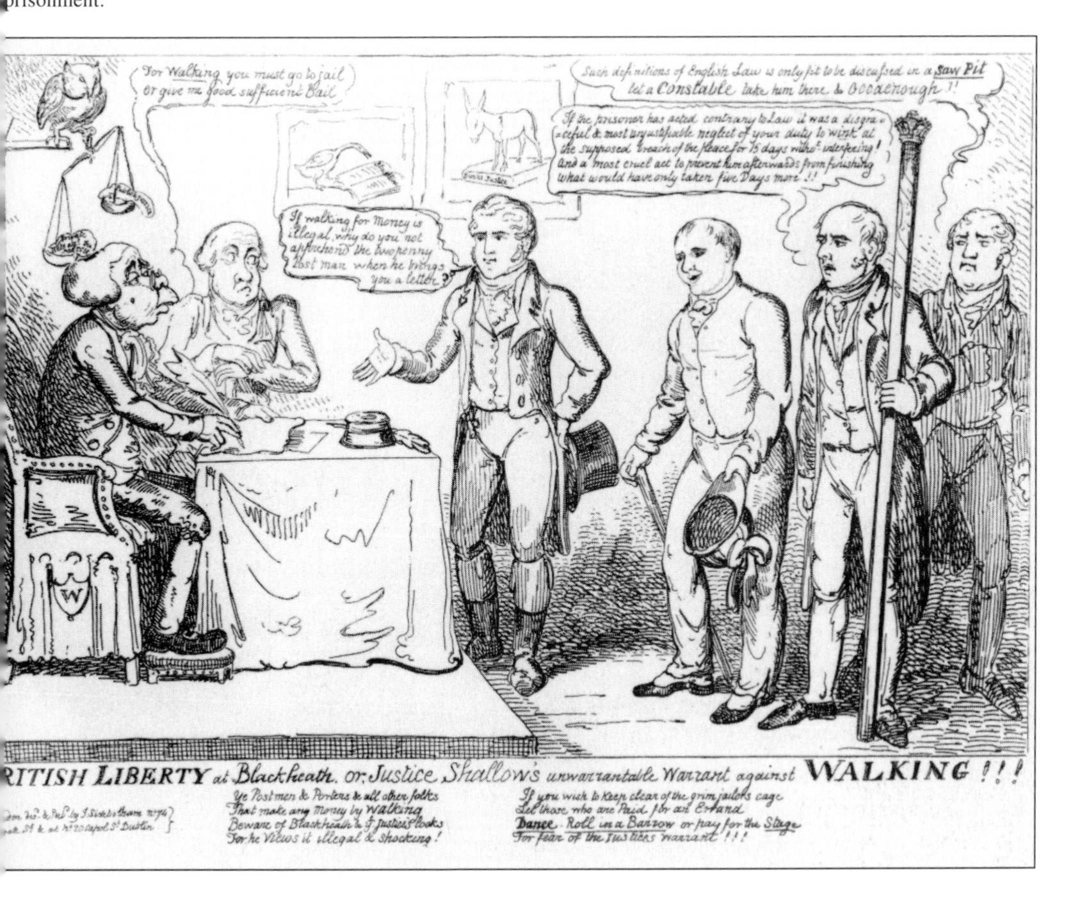

houses, and the Green Man hotel was the venue for balls and concerts, including, in 1834, one by the great Paganini himself. The wizard delighted his audience 'of a more select description and fashionable appearance than we ever witnessed in the room' by playing as an encore 'a few surprising and beautiful variations on *St Patrick's Day*' (source 45: 26 April 1834).

Life was not all sports and balls and concerts, however. In the 1820s and '30s an epidemic of burglary swept the district, and the chief targets were the detached houses of the rich, made vulnerable by the seclusion that was otherwise their chief advantage. In 1835, for example, a 'gang of juvenile burglars' lodging in the notorious slums of Mill Lane, Deptford (now Brookmill Road) ransacked houses in Blackheath, under the orders of the Fagin-like John Roberts of Deptford High Street, 'marine store dealer' (source 45: 26 December 1835).

The parish did not often make the national headlines, but in 1822 a bungled burglary escalated into 'the Lewisham Murder', which thrilled the country for months. The victim was James Smith, who lived in Morden Hill, probably at the old mill house. A gang of about six attempted to break in during the night and shot Mr Smith when he came to a window to investigate. There was nothing unusual in burglars and householders exchanging shots, but this case aroused particular horror because two of the gang (including the one alleged to have fired the shot) were nephews of the murdered man. The case throws light on the inadequate police arrangements so soon to be reformed by Sir Robert Peel. The watchman from Dartmouth Row, who arrived at the inquest drunk, admitted

> that it was ten minutes from the time he heard the report of firearms till he went to the house of the deceased; and on being asked why he did not go immediately to ascertain the cause, he said, perhaps he might have been shot too (source 4).

Little advance here on Dogberry and Verges.

Religion has always been looked to as a means of controlling the poor and taming the vicious. This is perhaps why Lewisham saw a burst of church building during the 1820s. The Congregationalists had revived their cause in Sydenham by building a new church there in 1819, and in 1823 they opened the Union Chapel in Lewisham High Street, where they had previously worshipped in an old brewery. Reformation of manners did not follow immediately, as it was probably this High Street building that was robbed by 'some desperate villains' in 1827. 'Every thing valuable was stolen, all the brass chandeliers were broken off, and every piece of brass that it was possible to remove was carried away' (source 4). The Methodists, who had a long tradition of open-air preaching in the parish, first acquired a fixed headquarters (in a room near Lewisham Bridge) in 1822, and they built their first church in Avenue Road in 1838.

The Church of England countered in 1824, when John Forster built a chapel of ease to serve his village of Southend. As the old dissenters' meeting house at Sydenham had been taken over by the Revd P.A. French as an Anglican proprietary chapel in 1794 or '95, this meant that residents of the two most remote parts of Lewisham had no longer to travel to St Mary's for worship. Nevertheless, Sydenham was still dissatisfied because accommodation at French's Chapel was limited and expensive, and according to Thomas Campbell the building was very cold and the sermons very dull.

In 1824 William Dacres Adams, the brother-in-law of the Mayow sisters of the Old House, began to campaign for a new church to be built at Sydenham, with the aid of money voted by Parliament. This was the origin of St Bartholomew's. Adams secured the goodwill of the Earl of Dartmouth and his uncle, the Bishop of Oxford, who was still Vicar of Lewisham. He then took his proposal to a meeting of the parish vestry to obtain a special church rate. The rest of the affair is a commentary on the first advice given to Adams by Lord Dartmouth: that if he planned to form a committee he should make it a very small one. At the meeting a member of the vestry suggested that while they were building one church they might as well make it two, and put the second on Blackheath. This was carried by acclamation and thereafter the churches were Siamese twins, so that the sickness and death of the Blackheath scheme was nearly fatal to St Bartholomew's. Problems arose because the vestry picked a site for the Blackheath church at the top of Lewisham Hill, midway between Dartmouth House and the home of the earl's uncle, Admiral Sir Arthur Legge, at the Knoll. The result was described in 1828 in a delightfully malicious paragraph headlined 'Ferment in the Parish of Lewisham':

artmouth Point, at the top of ewisham Hill, was the cturesque spot chosen by the estrymen as a site for their lackheath church. ortunately they were routed, nd this corner of the Heath is carcely less wild today.

> The Earl of Dartmouth, the Lord of the Manor of Blackheath [sic], being President of the Bible Society of that place, and in great odour of sanctity, it was never once imagined that he would hesitate to give a suitable piece of ground for the Church; but it happens unfortunately, that the erection of a Church on a suitable spot, would interrupt the delightful prospect from his Lordship's house, and the house of his neighbour, Sir Arthur Legge; and his Lordship, however anxious he might be to place the means of salvation within the reach of the inhabitants of Blackheath, was still more anxious to preserve his own prospect. He, however, it is true, exerted himself to procure a spot of ground elsewhere, but it was in the valley near the old Church, where, of course, an additional one was not wanted. The Commissioners having powers to appropriate wastes, the inhabitants applied to them to compel Lord Dartmouth to allow them a piece of waste ground on Blackheath; but the Commissioners, being as skilful in the affairs of this

> world as in those of the next, declined the invidious work. The indignant parishioners, at a Meeting on Friday se'nnight, came to the determination of building neither of the Churches, though some progress had been made in the erection of one, to the great regret of several tradesmen, builders, carpenters, etc. who, as might be expected, were full of enthusiasm for a work calculated to advance the cause of religion and to put money into their own pockets. It was even proposed that the correspondence with the Earl of Dartmouth and the Commissioners should be printed and circulated among the inhabitants generally; but the consideration of the expense deterred them from adopting a resolution to that effect (source 4).

Work was at a standstill for two years. Then the Blackheath project was given up, the Lewisham vestry washed its hands of the affair, and the commissioners finally completed St Bartholomew's in 1832, with the aid only of private contributions for furnishings and such finishing touches as the clock and the battlements.

Even the completion of St Bartholomew's did not restore harmony between Lewisham and Sydenham. The minister appointed to the new church was Thomas Bowdler, a nephew of the infamous expurgator. Despite his title of perpetual curate, Bowdler expected to enjoy an independent position. But St Bartholomew's was only a chapel of ease to St Mary's, and soon the Hon. Henry Legge, the new Vicar of Lewisham, was sending detailed instructions about services to be performed. Bowdler noted angrily on the back of Legge's letter: 'I wrote that I found I had not till now known my true position here, and now that I know it, I do not like it, being in fact too old to go comfortably in a check string' (source 67: A 71/30). It is surprising that Legge had time to interfere with Bowdler's work, for on Boxing Day 1830 St Mary's had been seriously damaged by fire, and most of the attention of the parish was absorbed by the problems of restoration.

St Bartholomew's, 'the New Church at Sydenham', drawn by the architect, Lewis Vulliamy. He contributed to the ill humour which plagued the whole project by quarrelling with the commissioners about the fencing of the churchyard.

Church building was one result of worries about the continued docility of the poor. The provision of elementary schools was another. The Church of England already had control of the existing foundations, those of Colfe and Stanhope, and the Sydenham village school established by Mary Mayow in 1815. In the new political world of the 1830s, when the Church seemed threatened on all sides by the evil armies of non-conformity, the orthodox gentry of the parish rallied to the defence of the establishment by helping it to secure the hearts and minds of the rising generation. Sydenham was first in the field with the St Bartholomew's National Schools in Kirkdale, which were opened in 1832, the year of the consecration of the church. In Lewisham High Street the St Mary's National Schools were built in 1833, on land given by the Earl of Dartmouth at the request of his brother, the vicar. The Anglicans enjoyed a near monopoly of the education of the poor for a decade or two before the rival British schools of the dissenters were able to offer much competition.

Despite disquieting social and political trends, Lewisham was now at its peak. The beauty of the village was greatly enhanced by its stream, thus described in about 1817:

> This long street lies upon a gradual descent from the South, and a stream of pure water, which rises above the town, is constantly running through it as far as the bridge, where it unites with the river Ravensbourne. This stream is pent up by various sluices, and forms little reservoirs in front of the houses on the outside of a broad foot-road, which in the summer season, when shaded by the overhanging groves of trees, has a very rural and pleasant appearance (source 35: p. 64).

To these natural attractions was added the charm of the many fine eighteenth-century houses in the High Street and Rushey Green, some of them noted in this description from 1838:

> A little to the south of the church . . . a fine panoramic view presents itself. On the north the church tower, through a break in the luxuriant wood, forms the chief feature of a beautiful landscape. To the westward is seen the PRIORY, the elegant castellated seat of John Thackeray, Esq., with its gothic windows of stained glass, and the rich surrounding scenery, including various objects of artificial ornament. Further southward is the mansion of Henry Stainton, Esq., and beyond it, in the distance, ROSENTHAL, the residence of Alexander Rowland, Esq. The eastern portion of the circle is filled up by the neat residence and grounds of John Castendeick, Esq. (source 46: p. 23).

Only one of the houses mentioned here still survives: Springfield, 'the mansion of Henry Stainton', which is now converted into shops.

s painting of about 1835 ifies the enthusiasm of the 8 description. The obvious ures are the sign of the rge Inn, and the tower of Mary's; and the High Street am and its bridges appear he left. Peeping through trees above the George are the chimneys of the of houses, then recently t, called Southfields, now 359 and 361.

The attraction of the populous districts of Lewisham and Sydenham was their almost rural character. Southend and Brockley (the modern Crofton Park) were at this time still genuine villages, with a few large houses, some farms and rustic inns, and at Southend the two water mills. The charm of Brockley depended on its village green, that of Southend on its ponds.

Sadly a peak implies an imminent decline, and Lewisham received its first serious warning of this in about 1836. Grove House in Lewisham High Street, once a haunt of John Wilkes, had become the home of the Allens late in the eighteenth century. They were a typical Lewisham family, solicitors in Clifford's Inn. In the mid-1830s, however, they did a most untypical thing, one until then unique. When Grove House became superfluous to their requirements they did not sell the estate as it stood, but knocked down the house, laid out a street across the large garden, and offered the land for sale in small building plots. The side road was a novelty, the first turning from the High Street to have been established for a thousand years or so. It was called Avenue Road, and was soon lined with terraces and pairs of houses which to the modern eye would appear quite smart and spacious. To the wealthy Lewisham resident of 1840 they were portentous: 'genteel villas' (as the advertisements called them), very obviously built with the lower middle class and the respectable working class in mind. During the 1840s, when it contained practically the only accommodation of this kind, Avenue Road fulfilled an important function as a point of entry to the village for many families which later moved on to much better roads. This estate had added 70 houses to Lewisham's total by 1843, and some 110 by 1863. The site of Grove House continues to be significant because, when Avenue Road (later Romer Avenue) and its offshoots were finally swept away, the Lewisham Centre was built in their place.

The fall of Grove House did not mark a clean break with Lewisham's past. It was a decade before another High Street mansion shared its fate, and for some years after 1836 new country houses continued to be built in the parish. The last were Blythe Hill House (designed by Samuel Teulon), in 1842, Stanstead Lodge, probably in the same year, Ravensbourne Park House in 1843, and Mountsfield in about 1845. Grove House was not exactly the writing on the wall, but it was a graffito on the fence.

osite: The Croydon Canal the south side of enham Bridge painted by Hodges *c.* 1830. The scene ired this anonymous sody in 1834: 'Reader! if e eye be again dimmed by ks or business, or thy brain louded by the smoke and ur of close rooms and vded streets – if thy mind istracted by cankering s and heart rending ousies, betake thyself, I ech thee, to Sydenham ge. Beautiful is the scene (source 45: 21 June 1834). *w*: This anonymous view rockley was painted in 3. The artist was standing north of the Brockley , and looking towards the re site of Crofton Park on. The man is walking his in that direction. The pond opposite Brockley Grove, h is the road branching off e right, in front of the

CHAPTER FIVE

Sewers and Steam (1840–1880)

In 1847 Lewisham could still be described as a village, containing 'many good houses and villas, the residences of wealthy merchants and tradesmen of the metropolis, who have been induced to settle here on account of the short distance from London, the salubrity of the air, and the beauty of the surrounding country' (source 2: I 621). Things were beginning to change, however, as was emphasized in that same year by the demolition of a second major High Street house, the Rookery. The agents of change were the railways, which were beginning to make Lewisham a practical home for a much wider spectrum of the middle class.

The first railway in the capital, the London and Greenwich, which opened in 1836, had a direct effect on the north of the parish, within reach of Deptford station, by stimulating development in the Lewisham Road area. The moral impact was far greater, for it proved what could be achieved by this miracle of speed, and all local landowners must have been greatly encouraged in their building schemes by the certainty that further lines could not be long delayed.

The tracks penetrated into Lewisham in 1839, when the Dartmouth Arms (now Forest Hill) and Sydenham stations were opened on the London and Croydon Railway. The response from the developers was prompt. At Forest Hill many middle class houses were built in London Road during the 1840s, and rapidly filled by bankers, stockbrokers and merchants. Between the stations Sydenham Park, built over the old Croydon Canal reservoir, also quickly developed as a prosperous middle class area, for the fares were far too high to encourage working class commuting. In 1849 a worried estate agent from one of the older suburbs complained to *The Builder* that:

> those parties who can afford it are beginning to move off a little way into the country, along the different lines of railway. I know three or four instances of this within the last twelve months. One party has gone to reside at Sydenham, from the neighbourhood of Cloudsley-square, Islington, and the other two to Penge, on the Croydon line, from Myddlelton-square (source 85: pp. 239–40).

e London and Croydon ilway in 1839. This drawing L.J. Wood shows the view thwards from the area ich is now the Devonshire ad Nature Reserve towards Dartmouth Arms station at est Hill, with the tower of Bartholomew's, Sydenham minent in the distance. The ises partially visible on the : were in the part of nstead Road called Eliza ce, now occupied by the est Hill Hotel and its ghbours.

Trains did not come to the village itself until 1849, when the North Kent company opened Lewisham and Blackheath stations, but nevertheless railway mania was as dominant a factor in the 1840s as motorway blight has been in more recent decades, though with a very different effect. Between 1839 and 1849 parliamentary committees were constantly debating the merits of rival schemes for extending the new transport into the heart of Kent, and the local communities were no less obsessed by the subject. Every interest group had its own idea about the best route and the best situation for the stations, and the clash of these incompatible desires delayed the provision of a service until 1849. The developers, though, were not deterred from building in anticipation of demand. The demolition of Grove House had coincided with the opening of the London and Greenwich Railway. The development of Avenue Road and its offshoots on the site proceeded throughout the 1840s, and was practically concluded by the time Lewisham station opened in 1849. Edward Legh of the Limes began to build on the outlying parts of his garden in the late 1840s. The first few houses in Limes Grove, and in the High Street to the south, were occupied by 1849.

The original Lewisham station was not in its present position, but by the railway bridge in the High Street. The building of the line did not involve widespread destruction because it followed the course of the Upper Kidbrook along the valley between Lewisham and Blackheath. One of its comparatively few victims was the old weather-boarded Plough, which had to be rebuilt a little to the south, and was briefly renamed the Railway Tavern. Another was a building known as the Manor House, once the home of John Dickens, father of the great Charles. The novelist is said by a normally reliable witness to have stayed there himself. Once the new service was in operation, building, especially in the north of the parish, increased at a great pace. In 1857 the Mid Kent line was laid along the Ravensbourne and Pool valleys, with stations at Ladywell, Catford Bridge and Lower Sydenham, and the building boom spread into those areas. It was to accommodate this line that Lewisham station was moved to its present position, and received the name of Lewisham Junction.

The impact of the railways is best illustrated by the statistics of population. In 1821 the total had been 8,185; in 1831 9,659; and in 1841 12,276. This last figure shows the effect of the London and Greenwich on the north of the parish and the London and Croydon on the south. By 1851 the opening of the North Kent railway had helped to raise the total to 15,064, but the real increase came in the next decade, for by 1861 (boosted additionally by the arrival of the Crystal Palace) the population was 22,808. Thereafter the total continued to rise steeply, to 36,525 in 1871 and to 53,065 in 1881. By that time the annual first class season ticket from Lewisham to London cost £12, and the second class £9. The action of the railways on population was not entirely one way, for there were many accidents in the early days. In 1857, for example, eleven people were killed and many injured in a crash between Lewisham and Blackheath. The victims were working people in the open third class carriages.

Some of the developments that followed the opening of Lewisham station were explicitly linked to that event, as in this paragraph from 1853:

> A new road is about to be formed direct from the Lewisham station of the North Kent line of railway to Blackheath, and we understand that the whole of the ground has been taken for the purpose of building thereon a superior class of villa residences. The advantage of the new road both to pedestrians and horses will be the avoidance of the hill in the direction of the Lewisham Grammar School (source 60: 27 August 1853).

Curiously, one of the early residents of Granville Park was that well-known railwayman Samuel Smiles, the author of *Self Help*. While the Earl of St Germans was busy here in the north of the village, Lord Dartmouth was beginning an even more grandiose scheme at Lewisham Park, which was planned along the lines of a great London square, with a private pleasure ground in the centre. It was a sad result of the decline of Lewisham during the later nineteenth century that few developments were completed on the generous scale originally envisaged. Rennell Street and Molesworth Street represented a less ambitious response to the railway stimulus. These lower middle class houses were built late in the 1850s on the old garden of the Roebuck Inn.

s artist's impression issued
about 1857) to advertise
.nville Park shows a superb
:ep of detached villas, but
he event semi-detached
ises were built on almost
the plots. The new Crystal
ace looms on the skyline,
St Margaret's, Lee, is in
middle distance. The end
Aberdeen Terrace appears
the left, and a part of the
oll – the house attributed to
orge Gibson – on the right.

The new roads in the village itself were mostly the work of the great private landlords. Further south, especially along Stanstead Road and what is now Brockley Rise, a different kind of development was being initiated. In quick succession the National Freehold Building Land Society, the Church of England and General Freehold Land Allotment Society, and the Conservative Freehold Land Society bought tracts of poor farmland, laid out roads, and divided the building plots among their members. These varied in their social position and length of purse, but in general the houses that resulted from the movement were far less grand than Lewisham Park, or even Molesworth Street. West Kent Park (between Stanstead Road, Brockley Rise and the Croydon railway) was an area of small terraces and cottages, not far above the level of a slum. It marks the degeneracy of the word 'park', which had previously been the preserve of quality housing developments. On the high ground on the eastern side of Brockley Rise a more spacious estate was laid out by the Conservative Land Society under the name of Brockley Hill Park. It was optimistically promoted as being 'near the Crystal Palace' (source 4), and the houses were intended to rally round a splendid new church; but the plots were only slowly taken up, the church never lifted its Gothic head, and in Lowther Hill and Duncombe Hill, as in Lewisham Park, ambition and quality slowly declined during half a century of halting growth.

In the 1860s (further stimulated, perhaps, by the lessening of the expense of road transport from the abolition of the turnpike trusts) new developments came thick and fast: Morley and Slaithwaite Roads, the College Park estate, Eastdown Park, Ladywell Park, Mount Pleasant Road, and Park Road (now Beacon Road) at Hither Green, another scheme that began with a bang and ended with a whimper. To accommodate them, much farm and garden land had to be sacrificed. Eastdown Park, for example, replaced part of the Lewisham Nursery, which closed in 1860 when the lease expired, and Mount Pleasant Road was named after the house of Abraham Constable, the Lewisham brewer, which was demolished in the same year.

The swelling population could not be adequately served by the converted cottages that had acted as shops until 1840. In or around that year, Frederick's Place, on the corner of Avenue Road, became the first terrace of purpose-built shops in Lewisham itself – there had probably been earlier ones at Blackheath – and others soon appeared alongside it, so that the area now fronted by the street market quickly established its importance as a commercial centre. It did not enjoy this predominance for long, however, for in 1855 one of the new goddesses of the age, Hygiene, was called as a witness in favour of a rival group of shops (in a passage which any writer would be delighted to quote, for the reason that formerly induced great ladies to employ dwarves as their attendants):

> It has been stated in the Report of the Sanitary Commission, that a large amount of sickness and disease is spread by parcels of goods and provisions being carried from bad drained and ill-ventilated premises into the dwellings of the middle and upper classes, whether for Consumption or other uses.

Another casualty of the 186[illegible] building boom was College Farm, which was the proper[illegible] of Trinity College, Greenwi[illegible] It was sometimes called Clark's Farm, after the last tenants. College Park (the present Clarendon Rise and offshoots) was built over the fields. The farmhouse in the High Street, seen here, was demolished, and Albion Ro[illegible] (now Way) formed across th[illegible] site.

> Impressed with the importance of the above fact the Proprietors of the Granville Terrace, near the Lewisham Railway Station, have built a Terrace of Superior Class Shops, which will enable the large and increasing inhabitants of the surrounding neighbourhood to obtain articles of consumption of the very best and wholesome quality at the lowest possible price. And to assist the different Shopkeepers to carry out this most desirable object . . . no expense [is] spared in securing to each Trade large and roomy premises, good ventilation, and a constant supply of water, all of which are so essential to the production and keeping of wholesome and nutritious food, together with the most perfect system of drainage, executed under and approved by the Honourable Commissioners of Sewers (source 60: 7 April 1855).

Granville Terrace (in the parish of Lee, but firmly part of the history of Lewisham) soon became better known as the High Pavement, and under the leadership of the Chiesman Brothers was to dominate Lewisham's shopping for a century.

The shadow that accompanied all these new houses and shops, blackest when the sun shone brightest, was an appalling stink. Lewisham was not singular in having stank since it was first inhabited by man, but until the 1840s there was sufficient space between the houses, and sufficient natural drainage, for the problem to be manageable and bearable. Now the combination of a rapidly rising population, the queasiness of civilization, and the panic caused by the cholera epidemic of 1848–9, made it bearable no longer. The great subject of local discussion and speculation in the 1840s had been railways; in the 1850s it was sewers.

At the beginning of the decade the responsibility for this work was vested in the Metropolitan Commissioners for Sewers. In the parish of Lewisham they decided to give priority to the drainage of Sydenham where, coincidentally, Edward Vitruvius Lawes, their chairman, was living. Not for long, though, for it was a far from healthy occupation, and Lawes died in 1852, at the age of thirty-five, shortly after the deaths of several of his colleagues. The sewers built under his direction in Sydenham had been a disastrous failure, and gave rise to an opposition movement called the Anti-Aggression Association, which complained that 'before the Commission came here, the old parish drains acted well, but now they had been taken out of the hands of the parish and received no attention at all' (source 60: 11 June 1853). The new sewers had been planned before the Great Exhibition, but were still being constructed when it became known that the Crystal Palace would be moved to Sydenham. The explosion of building produced by that news meant that the sewers were obsolete before they were completed. In 1853 one of the medical members of the Anti-Aggression Association, William Roberts, stated that:

> A patient whom he was attending . . . died in 72 hours from direct poison arising from the foul state of the sewers, and it was the very worst case of fever he had ever seen. Should an unhealthy season or very hot weather set in, he was of opinion that many of the inhabitants would be victims . . . In conclusion, he stated that the roads were at the present time covered with a quantity of black sewerage matter, which was of course very detrimental to health (source 60: 11 June 1853).

As a result, the exile of poor Lord Palmerston at the Home Office was made even more miserable by his having to deal with an irate deputation of Sydenham ratepayers.

The Sewer Commissioners, aloof in their Soho offices, were apt to meet all demands for improvement with 'a brief, unexplanatory, and positive refusal'. In 1856 some of their powers were transferred to the new district boards of works, and the engineers of the Lewisham board set about clearing up the mess. Professionals naturally paint the gloomiest possible picture in reports. If they are independent consultants they hope to obtain the resulting contract, and wish it to be a lucrative one; if they are employees they want to secure the largest possible budget and staff. But even allowing for this, the reports of the Lewisham Board of Works clearly show that the situation was very serious. It was discovered that:

> the whole sewage of Sydenham and Forest Hill overflowed from the numberless cesspools in those places, and found its way through the ditches near and adjoining Stanstead Lane, and (except such portion as was evaporated in its course) thence to the river Ravensbourne, creating the most intolerable and pestilential stench from Forest Hill to Catford Bridge, and polluting to a frightful extent the chief source of supply of the Kent Water Works . . . (source 64: for 1856, p. 21).

In the village itself the construction in 1855 of a sewer from St Mary's church to Bell Green was the major enterprise of this kind. It was an event of great practical and symbolic importance in the history of Lewisham. For centuries the chief distinguishing feature of the village (apart from its length) was the stream that flowed along the western side of Rushey Green and the High Street before falling into the Ravensbourne just above Lewisham Bridge. The stream rose on Springfield, the land that is now covered by the Catford Shopping Centre. In 1835 this field was bought by Henry Stainton, a wealthy iron merchant, who had lived since 1817 in a house at the northern end of Rushey Green, which, as a result of this purchase, came to be called Springfield. Stainton used the stream to create expensive ornamental waterworks in his garden.

The digging of the main sewer and a branch sewer in 1855–6 cut the bed of clay that retained the water in the pond and drained it all away. The stream ran dry and many of the trees on its banks died. Its pale ghost remains even today in the greens that adorn parts of the High Street and Rushey Green, and here the trees were eventually replaced by others less greedy of water. But the old charm and character of the village were irretrievably lost, and indeed, if it is possible to point to any one moment at which Lewisham ceased to be a village, this is that moment.

The symbolic importance of the event is what it reveals about the shifting balance of power in Lewisham. The accidental draining of Springfield ruined Henry Stainton's waterworks, and also 'the beautiful trout stream, forming a handsome sheet of water', which had been one of the chief attractions of the Priory in the High Street, the home of John Thackeray, the founder of the almshouses. Stainton and Thackeray had both died in 1851, but their heirs still occupied the houses, and Stainton's son immediately sued the Metropolitan and Lewisham boards of works to force them to restore his water. Thirty years earlier – ten years earlier, perhaps – no public authority would have dared to invade the property rights of such important landowners as the Staintons and Thackerays. Now the Master of the Rolls, fully in accord with the zeitgeist, ruled against property and in favour of utility. As a result the families abandoned all plans to improve the beauty of these estates, and began to look instead at ways of exploiting their building potential.

vid Williams Wire (01–60), Vestry Clerk of visham, an office ivalent, *mutatis mutandis*, he chief executive of a dern council. He lived at ne House, George Gibson's sterpiece. This caricature s issued in the run up to the 1 by-election at eenwich, in which Wire was ndly beaten by his fellow erman, David Salomons; he did later have the solation of becoming Lord yor of London.

For centuries, the affairs of Lewisham had been dominated by the great landowners, through their manor courts, their position as justices of the peace, and increasingly through the meetings of the parish vestry. Here, the resident magnates wielded a strong influence by the long tradition of their taking the lead, and because so many of those attending the meetings were their tenants. This began to change in the 1820s as the political passions of the reform era spilled over into local affairs. The quarrel over the Blackheath church was an early example of turbulence in the vestry, and by the early 1850s the assembly had come to be noted for violent language. The meetings were still controlled by the extremely conservative vicar, Henry Legge, and by David Williams Wire, the vestry clerk, but the vicar was apt to be denounced as a liar by Edward Legh and other friends of the people, and Wire was the object of a campaign of abuse over his alleged dictatorship.

A greater change took place in 1856, when the Lewisham Board of Works was established and began to carry out some of the duties previously exercised or neglected by numbers of authorities, mostly unelected. The changing composition of the population meant that although some of the early members of the board were landowners, more were shopkeepers or businessmen, who here enjoyed a position of equality with the gentry. Even if a member were the tenant of Samuel Forster, he could scarcely expect that consideration to influence the member's vote now that there were so many good shops and houses constantly on the market. In 1856, then, began the reign of the shopkeepers in the government of Lewisham, and here ended any slight influence that aesthetic considerations may ever have had on that government. From this point the watchwords were immediate convenience and short-term profit.

The board established its modest offices in a terraced house in Grove Place, which had been built on the site of Cole's lunatic asylum, at the north end of the present hospital site. The members even apologized for adding a porch, 'for convenience not ornament'. Extreme modesty, or else 'a lively recollection of the scenes that were wont to be enacted at the meetings of the open vestry', led to their excluding the public and press from their deliberations, until a series of protests and deputations eventually forced them to admit reporters. The protestors had been saying that the act establishing the board was 'an evil, and inapplicable to a rural parish like Lewisham' and that it might 'be necessary to exert themselves to get rid of it and fall back upon their own local act' (source 60: 13 December 1856). In 1857 the high-handed actions of the members had involved the board in a complication of legal disputes, but victories over Stainton on the Springfield question, over the New Cross Turnpike Trustees, whose roads had been damaged by sewer works, and over the owners of the Ravensbourne mills, whose water-power had been reduced by drainage measures, left them triumphant.

The offices of the Lewisham Board of Works, as built in 1874–5. An extension on the west side (left) later spoiled the proportions. The site had become parish property unde the terms of the enclosure award in about 1812, and as early as 1852 one of the loca political factions had a sche to build vestry offices here, because the meetings of that body at St Mary's had usuall to be adjourned to a larger room at the National School across the road.

In the 1870s the growing self-confidence, not to say importance, of the Board of Works was shown by the abandonment of Grove Place and the building of expensive Gothic offices, which were soon being called Catford Cathedral by the politically irreverent. At the same time, the members decided to print the minutes of their meetings for general edification. An incident resulting from this was recorded by the *Pall Mall Gazette*. The perfection of the paragraph is only marred by a hint of irony, a figure unsuited to the dignity of history, and elsewhere rigidly excluded from these pages.

> With a liberality rarely displayed by local bodies, the Lewisham district board of works at their last meeting rewarded their clerk for his services by a really magnificent present . . . a handsomely bound volume of the board's minutes and accounts for 1874. The volume was surmounted by the Board's 'coat of arms' and bore an inscription in gold stating that it was presented to the clerk in recognition of 'the care and ability bestowed by him in compiling and editing this the first volume of the printed minutes of their proceedings'. The chairman in presenting this valuable gift addressed a few feeling words to the clerk, who, when he had overcome his emotion, made a touching reply. 'The handsome present,' he said, 'was in itself of no specific value, as he had always the minutes before him; but as a mark of the board's appreciation of his labours he valued it highly, and should always look upon the inscription with gratification and pleasure'. . . The labour of compiling the precious volume had evidently exhausted the clerk for the moment, and rendered him unable at first to realize the full value of the priceless treasure of which he is now the fortunate possessor. Should he, however, continue to be of opinion that the gift has 'no specific value' Government will no doubt gladly enter into negotiation for its purchase, with the view of depositing it in the British Museum (source 86).

The various organs of government had much to do during the busy decades of the mid-century. In 1855, the year when the High Street stream ran dry, the rural aspect of the village was further altered by the introduction of gas lighting, which the conservative element in Lewisham had resisted for longer than in any of the neighbouring areas. At a meeting to consider the question, the decisive argument, advanced by James Belcham, the linen draper, was that 'the commercial prosperity of the parish would be improved'. It was agreed to erect gas lamps from the Sydney Arms in Lewisham Road to Rosenthal in Rushey Green, and they were expected to 'afford great convenience to the inhabitants of this hitherto benighted locality' (source 60: 13 January 1855).

The medical officers appointed by the board of works acted quickly to suppress the threats to health posed by poor drainage, inadequate water-supply and noxious trades. Provision for the sick was slower to develop, with the nearest hospitals, until the 1870s, being still in London. The first to open in Lewisham parish was the cottage hospital set up by the board of works in Verdant Lane in 1871. It was intended specially for cases of fever, and treatment was restricted to those (mainly servants) for whom someone was willing to pay. For most of the poor, the only resort was to the sick ward of the workhouse. The rich were nearly always treated at home, even in the gravest cases.

The pauper insane were usually sent to the Kent county asylum at Barming Heath near Maidstone (opened in 1833), for which the parishes had helped to pay through a lunatic rate. For the wealthy there were the private madhouses, including James Cole's at Dartmouth House, Lewisham, at the north end of the present hospital site, which was demolished in 1861. If we could only know the life stories of his patients they would probably tell us more about the realities of Victorian life than many a ponderous textbook. This, and the workhouse, stood as a dual warning in the centre of the village of the dangers of financial and emotional irresponsibility.

The second hospital in Lewisham was the Home an[d] Infirmary for Sick Children, [a] private charity financed by t[he] middle classes of Sydenham for the benefit of the poor. It[s] first home, from 1872 until 1885, was at 5 and 6 Albion Villas Road, seen here in the 1870s. The pair had been bu[ilt] in about 1847 as private houses, and it has since returned to domestic use.

It might seem that even the dead were not forgotten by the new brooms of local government, though in truth the cemetaries movement had more to do with hygiene than with piety. The graveyard of St Mary's, even after enlargements in 1791 and 1817, and even after burials began at St Bartholomew's at Sydenham in 1832, was inadequate to the needs of the growing town. Ladywell Cemetary, laying out since 1856, was opened in 1858, and burials at the churches ceased, except in existing family vaults.

The Lewisham police station moved in the early 1850s from its first site, opposite George Lane, to a house just north of the Black Horse in Rushey Green, and again in the mid-1870s to one opposite Ladywell Road. All three were existing buildings converted to that use. The first purpose-built police station was the one at Sydenham, on part of the present site, which was opened in 1848.

There was much for the police to do, as the enlarged population produced a fair crop of native offenders, and Lewisham's prosperous houses proved an irresistible lure for gangs of housebreakers from far and near. It is striking how often these burglaries involved the use of firearms. In 1880, for example:

> a burglar, while plundering the house of a Bank of England clerk, was interrupted by one of the inmates, and, after a desperate struggle, escaped. His assailant's night-dress was shot through, but a parting bullet struck the burglar as he was passing over the lawn, without, however, preventing him getting clear off (source 4).

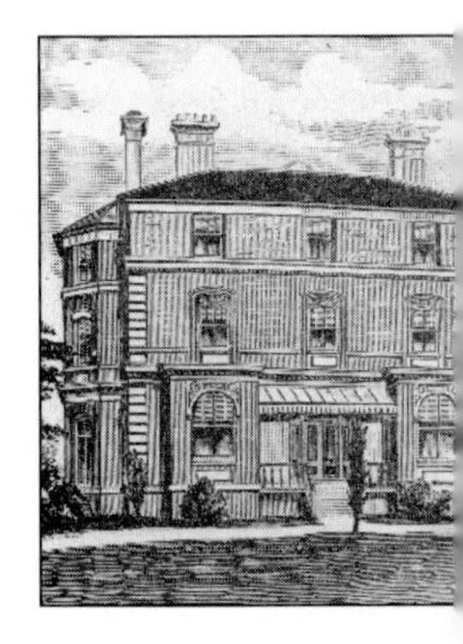

This was Champion Hall, th[e] second and final home of th[e] children's hospital. It was in Sydenham Road, not far fro[m] Bell Green, and had been bu[ilt] in 1861. Over a century the original house was extende[d in] all directions, and largely hidden from view, but it survived until the closure of the hospital, which was demolished in 1991.

A far more amusing crime or misdemeanour – for posterity, at least – took place at the Lewisham North post office, which was run by James Lindsay in a shop next door to the Joiners' Arms. In 1844 Mrs Lindsay's maid left her to marry a builder's foreman. When, shortly afterwards, the husband was writing a letter, his bride advised him on no account to post it at Lindsay's. In explanation, she said that Mrs Lindsay had long been in the habit of opening all the letters passing through that office and reading them, often with the help of her maid in deciphering a difficult hand. Where possible she resealed the letters and sent them on, otherwise she burnt them, but in either case she rapidly transmitted this authentic gossip about love affairs and family scandals all round the village. Lewisham was in an uproar. A crowded public meeting was held at the Lion and Lamb, the local 'Jupiter' thundered in an editorial, and angry correspondence was exchanged (not, presumably, via Lindsay's) with St Martin's-le-Grand; but in the upshot Lewisham's Paulina Pry at the post office received no worse punishment than the removal of the franchise from her husband's shop, and the hatred of all her neighbours.

This demoralization and laxity was accompanied by a great burst of church building. All the denominations joined in and, as far as their means permitted, all built in the same style. As it was a drab and gloomy style, the regret that a number of these churches were to be destroyed in the Blitz need not be too intense. The Anglicans were most active in the fast-growing districts of Sydenham and Forest Hill. In Lewisham itself they founded St Stephen's in the High Street in 1865, and St Mark's in Clarendon Road (now Clarendon Rise) in 1870. At Blackheath the Church of England built All Saints' church in 1857, this time with the cordial cooperation of the Earl of Dartmouth of the day, from whose houses it was respectfully distant. The Congregationalists, Baptists and Methodists built a great many churches all over Lewisham during these decades, but twentieth-century warfare and irreligion have left comparatively few of them standing.

Provision of places of public resort in Lewisham was slow to develop. It was probably delayed by the close neighbourhood of the Crystal Palace, an entertainment centre of international renown. Although its new site after the Great Exhibition proved to be just outside the Lewisham boundaries, the palace was always spoken of as 'at Sydenham' and had a profound effect on the development of that village. In 1858 it was said that:

> the great event in the history of Sydenham was the selection of the hill above it as the site for the Crystal Palace, the first column of which was raised on the 5th of August 1852. Magnificent, and at first, alas! too visionary, were the anticipations of the promoters of this grand enterprise. The Crystal Palace was to be the nucleus of a new metropolis. Here, in

The Crystal Palace in its firs splendour, as seen from the low level station. The splendour owes something tc artistic licence, as the fountains were unable to pla with any effect until Brunel had completed his replaceme water towers in 1856, and th north tower does not appear this engraving. The north transept, in the centre of the picture, was burnt down in 1866, and never replaced.

> fact, was to be New London;– that Old London, viewed seven miles away from the summit of the hill, was to be venerated as a relic of the past (source 18: pp. 5–6).

Three of the leading figures in the Crystal Palace Company, Samuel Laing, Thomas Newman Farquhar and John Scott Russell, had been residents of Sydenham since the 1840s, and they were no doubt largely responsible for the choice of the new location.

The Crystal Palace stimulated building all over Sydenham and Forest Hill to such an extent that in 1871 (for the only time in a census year) the population of Sydenham and Forest Hill, at 19,065, was higher than that for all the rest of the parish, where there were 17,460 people. In 1851 the population of Sydenham and Forest Hill had been a mere 4,501, so it had more than quadrupled in twenty years. The price of building land in Sydenham was about £610 per acre in 1854, when in Lewisham village it was only £360. The effect of the Crystal Palace was naturally most dramatic in and around Westwood Hill and Sydenham Hill. The Forsters of Southend, and most of the other owners of this high ground, had resisted the temptation to build after the enclosure of the common, when the market was glutted, and they were to receive a rich reward for their patience. Some of the houses now built on Sydenham Hill were palatial, but showed little regard for consistency of style.

> The merchants in the sixties liked the view,
> and came to stay, their prospects being good,
> their credit high, with markets vast and new . . .

So architects possessed of taste and skill
set out to choose a dozen styles from stock
and then combine them, at their clients' will

Italian, Tudor, Gothic, and Baroque . . .

(Bernard Bergonzi)

Edward FitzGerald called Sydenham 'a wonderful museum of hideous Cockney Villas' (source 38: III 362). The area seems to have had a particular attraction for tea merchants. Horniman and the Tetleys settled at Forest Hill, and St Margaret's in Sydenham Hill (now no. 12) was built for another, Thomas Ross.

The finest of the new districts created during the Crystal Palace building boom of the 1850s and '60s was the Lawrie estate (between Westwood Hill and Crystal Palace Park Road), which George Wythes, later the developer of Bickley, turned into something resembling Kensington at its most expansive.

The new residents of Sydenham and Forest Hill included a sprinkling of aristocrats, many senior army officers, and a number of writers, actors, painters and musicians. An important factor in attracting artists to the district was the reputation of the Crystal Palace concerts, for the band was then the most skilful and enterprising in the country. The credit for this was due to Sir George Grove, the secretary of the Crystal Palace Company, who lived at the present 14 Westwood Hill from 1852 until 1860, and afterwards near Bell Green; and to August Manns, the conductor, one of whose homes was Athol Lodge, now no. 174 Kirkdale. This musical fame was no doubt also one of the features that attracted so many Germans to the area, and that tendency led to (and was in turn further stimulated by) the establishment of a Lutheran church there in 1875. This was one of fifteen or more churches built by the various denominations in Sydenham and Forest Hill between 1854 and 1880.

Philip's church in Taylor's ne, Sydenham, was built tween 1865 and 1867, to the signs of Edwin Nash, a stinguished architect who ed successively in denham Park, and in Border ad, Lawrie Park, and may ve had a hand in the shaping both those estates. His etch of the church, which lly was to be demolished in 82, was published in 1867.

Sir Joseph Paxton's masterpiece, which called so much of Sydenham into being, has gone, alas, and with it much of the charm and prosperity of the area. Rockhills, the house adjoining the Crystal Palace, which the great gardener enlarged and embellished for his own use, did not survive much longer. But Sydenham can still boast two buildings designed in part by Paxton. The Wood, no. 16 Sydenham Hill, was occupied from 1855 by Lady Hunloke, the old mistress of Sir Joseph's patron, the sixth Duke of Devonshire. The 'Bachelor Duke' was a frequent guest at Rockhills, and there was constant intercourse between the two houses. It is certain that the Cavendish millions financed the lavish extensions to the Wood during the 1850s, and practically certain that Paxton designed them.

The Wood in the late 1850s. The figures in the backgrour may be the Duke of Devonshire and Paxton. In t foreground are almost certainly Anne, Lady Hunloke, and her daughter Charlotte – 'the fat ladies' a the two men had dubbed the with old world courtesy.

The Forest Hill Boys' Industrial Home in Rojack Road shortly after it was founded in 1873. The girls' home was opened in the sam street in 1881. The former moved to Shaftesbury House in Perry Rise in 1883, the lat to Louise House in Dartmou Road in 1891. The children were mostly orphans or from broken homes. The girls wer prepared for domestic servic the boys trained as shoemakers.

His other surviving local work is the Sydenham Public Lecture Hall (now the Kirkdale Centre), which was originally intended to be a miniature imitation of the Crystal Palace until changes in the London building laws forbad anything in that style. Paxton then donated designs for a more conventional hall, which were adapted by Henry Dawson because the full scheme could not be afforded at once. The lecture hall was officially opened by Paxton himself in 1861.

It was one of several initiatives of the 1860s and '70s designed to improve the lot of the poor in Sydenham and Forest Hill, whose wretchedness had been thrown into sharper contrast by the increasing prosperity of most of the inhabitants. Other schemes were the Home and Infirmary for Sick Children, in 1872, and the Forest Hill

Industrial Home, in 1873. St Matthew's church in Panmure Road was opened in 1879 specifically as a mission to the poor, who were believed to be intimidated by the splendour of the congregation at St Bartholomew's, 'one of the great prizes of the Church', which had more than once 'lain in the road to a Bishopric' (source 11: VI 144).

Concern about charities – though not necessarily about the poor – was very widespread in the 1850s, when packs of John Bolds roamed the land sniffing out corruption. In Lewisham one who signed himself 'A Studious Traveller' took delight in poisoning the lives of the officials of the Leathersellers' Company by criticizing their administration of Colfe's Library, which had been intended for the use of the public, but which, in course of time, had become a purely private adjunct to the grammar school.

Reformers in the Lewisham Vestry next exploited a far more promising vein of discontent by attacking the administration of Colfe's Grammar School itself. In 1855 George Weedon Bennett, the Blackheath clockmaker, moved for an enquiry into Colfe's charities. He told the meeting that:

> He had not himself been educated in the grammar-school, but his brother had, and he could tell them that boys on the foundation were looked on as paupers. One reason given was that the foundation was so small, that the master was allowed private pupils, and it was considered infra dig for these to associate with the other pupils. He could not bring himself to think that Colfe meant there should be anything of this kind. (hear) (source 60: 31 March 1855)

The Hon. and Revd Henry Legge came in for some sharp attacks at this meeting. Edward Legh of the Limes, in declining to serve on a committee with Legge, said that the master of Colfe's English School had been left almost entirely unsupervised, and Legh was grieved to find that 'during the period of eleven years the vicar of their parish, who was specially named in Colfe's will, had only found leisure to attend twice, and then but for a period of five or ten minutes'. John Bennett, the old Colfeian (later Sir John), remarked that, 'If it was the vicar's opinion that the people might know too much, he was welcome to his opinion; but they, believing in the spread of education, should not stand there and play the hypocrite' (source 60: 31 March 1855).

This was late in the headmastership of Joseph Prendergast, a man of whom one saddle-sore pupil remarked, 'to say the least of it he was a brute'. His quarrels with the Leathersellers' Company had already embroiled the school in Chancery, and it continued to be tossed about between that court and the Charity Commission until a new constitution was finally agreed in 1887.

Dartmouth chapel in about 1840, shortly after the second rebuilding. The watercolour is captioned 'Miss Stone's Chapel', because Perceval House, next door, was then occupied by Sapientia Stone's school, and her boarders probably formed the major part of the congregation.

Another target for the reformers was the Blackheath chapel, and this provided an opportunity for baiting the vicar's kinsmen, the fourth and fifth earls of Dartmouth. Susannah Grahme's gift had been left to trustees, who included her nephew, the first Lord Dartmouth. Eventually the management fell entirely into the hands of the earls, who continued to pay the vicars of Lewisham (often members of their own family) for conducting the services. The chapel was rebuilt in 1750 and again in 1838, and from 1750 the earls reimbursed themselves for the building expenses by charging pew rents, which became a regular part of the income from their Lewisham estate. In 1852 various local reformers began to agitate for the free use of the chapel by the public, and in 1855, after some superficial historical research, which failed even to establish the relationship of Mrs Grahme to the Legge family, the Master of the Rolls decided against Lord Dartmouth. The chapel was thus set on the road to becoming the centre of an independent parish in 1883, as the Church of the Ascension.

This harrassing of the rich was very enjoyable, no doubt, but meanwhile the real interests of the poor were as much neglected as usual. The regime at Lewisham workhouse became notorious for its harshness (which led to a serious scandal in 1853), and the choice of officers seems to have been guided more by humour than compassion: in 1878 the master and matron were Mr William and Mrs Harriet Want. There was a regular conspiracy between the Guardians of the Poor and the Charity Organization Society to scare away applicants for relief, which involved the latter suspending 'in the public street outside its office a list of the names of persons receiving outdoor relief' (source 4).

This society 'employed an officer, whose business it was to patrol the neighbourhood, warning off beggars, and, when necessary, giving them into charge of the police. Much useful work conducive to the comfort of the inhabitants was done by this officer . . .' (source 60: 4 March 1882). The local papers of the last three decades of the century are full of complaints about street begging, especially by children.

The harsh morality of the new Lewisham was increasingly mirrored by its appearance. A former resident, James Thorne, writing in 1876, says that 'Lewisham was only a few years ago a pleasant rural district, but it has fallen a prey to the builder, and has become much like any other suburban village' (source 104: II 417). The quality of the builders now preying on the parish is suggested by this item from 1879:

> Mr Champion, a 'speculative Builder' at Lewisham, has recently been somewhat unfortunate in business. In six weeks he erected a block of six houses [in Harvard Road], three of which almost immediately fell down, and now the magistrates have ordered him to pull down the remaining three, lest they also should fall of their own accord. The materials were said to be bad, but one witness declared them to be 'quite good enough for speculative building'. Perhaps, however, it is as well for Mr Champion that the houses collapsed before being tenanted (source 4).

A shoddy age was beginning.

CHAPTER SIX

Metropolitan Improvements? (1880–1914)

The two decades from 1880 to 1900 were those of Lewisham's most striking transformation. An average modern citizen of the town, if suddenly dropped into the High Street of 1880, would be bewildered, with very few landmarks he could recognize; but if taken back to 1900 instead he would feel comparatively at home. Those years saw the destruction of nearly all the remaining large houses in the High Street and Rushey Green, the rebuilding of most of the old public houses, and the creation of four department stores in central Lewisham. They also saw the loss of nearly all the remaining farmland in the parish. Only a doomed agricultural fringe in the south-west struggled on into the 1920s.

Population figures tell the dramatic story. In 1881 there were 53,065 people in the parish of Lewisham; in 1891, 72,272; in 1896, 83,213; and in 1901, 108,846. The numbers had doubled in twenty years, a rate of increase not approached since then.

There was little industry in Lewisham by this time, and the majority of the new families were headed by commuters to the City of London, or to the factories of Bermondsey, Greenwich, Woolwich and the like. Most could only afford to live in suburbia when cheap travel became available, so the key to the especially huge influx of the 1890s is to be found in improved transport. The railways continued to play their vital part, with several new lines and stations. The long expected opening of Hither Green in 1895 had a tremendous impact on the development of that quiet and, until then, rather select area; and Bellingham station (1892) encouraged building on the Forster estate along the Bromley Road. Carefully organized horse buses had long been replacing the old coaches with something approaching a modern service, but the great new agents of change, highly important both in driving out the old residents and bringing in the new, were the horse trams.

Vague schemes for bringing trams to Lewisham or Forest Hill had been aired since the 1870s, and during the '80s there were numerous applications for lines, and enquiries about their desirability. The South-Eastern Metropolitan Tramways Company had plans for an extensive network in Lewisham, but local opposition eventually reduced this to a single service from Rushey Green to Greenwich, where there was access to London trams. The lines were laid down with great haste in the summer of 1890. The service was, from the first, cheaper than the rival forms of transport, but things were carried an important stage further in 1895 when the Lewisham Board of Works (previously very dubious about trams) requested the provision of workmen's cars. The company immediately agreed to schedule two, to leave Catford at 5.30 and 6.30 in the morning, and announced 'that the fare would be one penny any distance' (source 65: 1895/6, p. 142).

The rich accepted the first creak of a tram wheel outside their gates as notice to quit. There had been a steady leakage of wealthy residents in the 1880s, often to places on the Brighton line, like Redhill and Burgess Hill. In the '90s the leak became a flood, for once started, it accelerated automatically. The large houses that fell vacant proved hard to let and tended to be bought by developers. The small houses they built persuaded the owners of the adjoining estates that it was time to move on, and soon there were scarcely any large houses left. The trend is neatly captured in the advertisements of estate agents, who passed from 'highly desirable country residence' via 'would alternatively provide an eligible site for development' to 'prime development site, also including' (in very small print) 'an old-fashioned family house'.

In 1879 Lewisham had acquired a vicar, Augustus Legge, who was a curious mixture of the old and the new: old because he was the son of the fourth Earl of Dartmouth, and the last of his family to follow this traditional route to a mitre; new because he was an energetic clergyman in the most approved late Victorian manner. The parish organization of St Mary's in his day was as different as possible from 'the old-fashioned *régime* of a previous vicar' (his uncle and predecessor Henry Legge) 'who lived on Blackheath, and, we are told, visited the parish with his pockets full of half-crowns and packets of tea in fulfilment of his duties there' (source 11: VI 147). Reviewing the years from 1880 to 1883, Augustus Legge recalled that:

> The quiet and . . . lazy village was bursting into a populous town; the older houses, with their extensive grounds, were beginning to make way, one by one, for the rows of streets which multiply the population tenfold in as many years; the open fields were, some of them, already being

> intersected with new roads, whilst in most of those that remained big boards announced in red or black that the land was to be let for building (source 96: 1880–3, p. 3).

In 1884 he wrote:

> The process referred to in my last letter, by which the houses and grounds, which were once the pride of the village, make way for rows and rows of cottages, goes on with increasing rapidity. The destruction of the Priory with its pleasant associations . . . is following in the wake of that of Springfield. Rosenthal is threatened with a like fate; and the removal of the Hubbucks deprives us of one more of those families who were always ready to employ the means at their disposal for the promotion of the welfare of their neighbours. These changes cannot but be subjects of regret. They affect the whole community. Trade suffers; the number of persons dependent on daily wages increases; employment diminishes. There is more poverty and consequent suffering; there are fewer who are able to contribute substantially to its relief (source 96: 1884, p. 3).

In the old Lewisham most of the houses had been owned by the local magnates. The thousands built at the end of the nineteenth century were more likely to have been acquired as an investment by small capitalists living in any part of the country. One of the many who owned houses in the town was Samuel Butler, the author of *Erewhon* – a rare instance of Lewisham supporting the arts.

The local market was still well stocked with the large houses built between 1845 and 1875, so most of the new ones during the remainder of the century were designed (or at any rate constructed) with working or lower middle class tenants in mind. In 1902 it was

The Priory in about 1824, during the early years of Jo Thackeray's occupancy. Thi is the front of the house, see from a spot which in moder terms would be near to the corner of Roxley Road.

reported (from the information of a Catford builder) that 'Folks, belonging more especially to the artisan class, have come out from Camberwell and Peckham, and in numerous instances delight has been expressed with the more pleasant conditions that suburban life affords in this locality' (source 66: 21 August 1902).

Only a few of the countless developments need be mentioned. The year 1880 was a watershed, with a phenomenal 655 new houses being started in the parish. During the '80s much of the land to the west of Rushey Green (formerly the grounds of the Priory, Springfield, Elmwood, and Ravensbourne Lodge) was covered by Brookdale Road, Albacore Crescent, Doggett Road and many others. Between Brownhill Road and Sangley Road the estate comprising Plassey Road, Engleheart Road, Bowness Road and Jutland Road was being built in 1881. The Leathersellers' Colfe estate, south of Stanstead Road, was another large development of the '80s, and that decade also saw considerable building – of instant slums for the most part – around Bell Green. Nearby is Fairlawn Park, which illustrates the social changes in the area towards the end of the century. The name and layout of this estate makes the smallness of the houses surprising. The discrepancy arose because the churchwardens of St Olave's, Southwark, the trustees of the land, had decided to build as early as 1843, and set out the basic road pattern not long afterwards. In 1869 they agreed with a developer to the construction of eighty houses at a cost of £400 each. He completed the roads and sewers, but could find no clients for houses of that size – now that the gas company was making its distinctive contribution to the quality of life at Bell Green – and had built none by 1880. He then asked for modified terms and was allowed to build a larger number of houses at a cost of £250 each. Work began at once, and eventually about 165 houses and shops were squeezed in.

Two areas planned and laid out in the 1890s, but largely built early in the twentieth century, were the Bridge House farm site to the south of Ladywell Road, and the St Germans (or Corbett) estate at Hither Green. The latter was a huge undertaking, with more than twenty new roads covering 278 acres of the Earl of St Germans's farmland. Archibald Cameron Corbett, MP, a second generation building developer of Scottish ancestry and strict teetotal and Presbyterian beliefs, bought the freehold from the earl in 1896. Within five years he had built nearly two thousand houses, and he sold them almost immediately at the rate of two a day – excluding Sundays. When finally completed shortly before the Great War, the estate comprised some three thousand houses and had added more than fifteen thousand to the population of Lewisham.

The Corbett estate marked a slight change from the 1880s' trend towards working class housing, for as well as many small terraced properties, Corbett built a number of substantial houses on the main roads, obviously aimed at the middle classes. This swing of the pendulum lasted throughout the Edwardian era. The 'Thorpe' estate at Sydenham and the Forster estate along Bromley Road were others that featured houses markedly superior to the average products of the previous two decades.

The physical changes in Lewisham (or surprising lack of them) were frequently remarked on during this period. Towards the end of the century the unromantic Charles Booth was moved to say:

> the impression left is still that of the main street in some small old-fashioned provincial town; low buildings, tiled roofs and quaint gables; and even the horse cars of the tram-line do not destroy the illusion as, jingling by at infrequent intervals, they pass through 'long and lazy Lewisham' (source 11: VI 150).

Other contemporaries agreed that Lewisham still offered that ever elusive suburban ideal, the 'admixture of country life with metropolitan conveniences'. But the last word belongs to the author of Murray's *Handbook for Travellers in Kent*, who reported in 1892 that 'the long straggling town of Lewisham stretches for a considerable distance along the high road to Sevenoaks, but contains nothing of interest' (source 82: p. 177).

Sir Arthur Conan Doyle, who knew Lewisham well, sent Sherlock Holmes and Dr Watson to the town in 1898 to investigate the case of Josiah Amberley, *The Retired Colourman*. Watson reports that:

> 'The Haven is the name of Mr Josiah Amberley's house . . . I think it would interest you Holmes. It is like some penurious patrician who has sunk into the company of his inferiors. You know that particular quarter, the monotonous brick streets, the weary suburban highways. Right in the middle of them, a little island of ancient culture and comfort, lies this old home, surrounded by a high sun-baked wall mottled with lichens and topped with moss, the sort of wall . . .'
>
> 'Cut out the poetry Watson,' said Holmes severely. 'I note that it was a high brick wall' (source 27: p. 1321).

Amberley had 'made his little pile, retired from business at the age of sixty-one, bought a house at Lewisham, and settled down to rest after a life of ceaseless grind'. In many respects he was typical of the thousands of London businessmen who settled in Lewisham in the nineteenth century, though comparatively few of them asphyxiated their wives.

Although Lewisham was losing wealthy residents and acquiring poor ones, the town was still remarkably prosperous. Between 1886 and 1889 Charles Booth estimated the standard of living in each district of London and found that Lewisham (with which he included Penge) had a lower percentage of poor, and a higher percentage of comfortably off inhabitants than Kensington, than Chelsea, than the parish of St George's, Hanover Square. In fact the only district better in these respects than Lewisham was Hampstead, and in Booth's top category (middle class and above) Lewisham had the highest proportion of all, with 37.4 per cent compared with 34 per cent for Hampstead, and an average of 17.8 per cent for London as a whole. Lewisham's decline was not at this period into poverty, but into a dull uniformity of lower middle class and artisan respectability. This was reflected in the small number of really eminent people who chose to live in the town.

Returning in 1902, Booth found that:

> In Lewisham, more perhaps than anywhere else, we find a new population overwhelming the old. The rich have gone. Clerks and commercial travellers, themselves divided into several classes, have taken their place; and below them there is a great and growing population of wage-earners . . . The new houses in St Mary's parish are intended for lower middle rather than working class, and, on the other hand, there is an entire absence of wealth . . . (source 11: VI 146, 150).

On the new estates at Hither Green and Catford the population consisted of 'clerks and artisans, mainly the former'. The 1901 census showed that Lewisham had a higher percentage of commercial clerks than any other part of London.

Sydenham was generally a very prosperous area, but Booth found that the parish of St Michael's was the exception:

> Poverty goes with crowding, and Bell Green is the one really poor district in this quarter of London . . . The people are thus described: 'gas-workers of all kinds, carmen, porters, painters, jobbing gardeners, roadmen, costermongers, laundresses, and a very large proportion of casual labourers; working-class almost exclusively, and many of them very poor. Ninety per cent of them would feel the pinch of a week's loss of wages' (source 11: VI 145).

The local job market was changing. Between 1880 and 1918, for the first time since the decline of water power at the end of the eighteenth century, industry began to return to the town. In Lewisham itself factories were established during these decades by, among others, George Harvey, the galvanizer (and radical candidate for the borough), Elliott Brothers, the instrument makers, and S.W. Farmer, the metalworker. At Catford there was James Robertson's preserve works, at Hither Green King's biscuit factory, and at Sydenham the works of the Crystal Palace Electric Supply Company.

For those not tempted by any of these job opportunities, the fact of so many young couples living on the Corbett estate at Hither Green opened up another avenue of gainful employment:

The biscuit works of T.O. Ki
and Son seen from an
imaginary elevation
somewhere above Hither
Green station, in about 1920.
The office in Staplehurst Roa
(on the right) had been built i
1913 as the highly
unsuccessful Globe Cinema,
and the first section of the
factory had been the
auditorium. The name of the
business was soon changed t
Chiltonian Biscuits, and in
1930 the operation was move
to Lee.

> The typical local offence is afternoon housebreaking, when the man is away and the wife goes out, leaving the house empty. It is difficult to prevent or to detect. Having quickly forced the lock, the impudent invader deceives any chance onlooking neighbour by a hearty greeting of an imaginary person within before the door closes, and the same simple formalities are repeated on his exit with the 'swag' (source 11: VI 148–9).

The Guardians of the Poor conferred a substantial benefit on the town in 1894 by building the Lewisham Infirmary. It was intended primarily for the sick and aged inmates of the adjoining workhouse, but from the first it admitted non-pauper patients. In the best traditions of political opposition, the progressive or radical minority criticized the infirmary as an expensive folly, but Lewisham Hospital has proved them wrong by completing a century of valuable service. This was not the first general hospital in Lewisham, for St John's in Morden Hill had been founded in 1885.

These decades produced an astonishingly rich crop of sports clubs, some making use of the parks, but many establishing private grounds, which helped to restict the intensity of building development. In the years around 1900 Lewisham was fleetingly a paradise for the lover of sport, with a sufficient, and sufficiently young and prosperous, population to maintain innumerable clubs, but still with enough open space for their grounds and pitches. This status was confirmed by the residence in Sydenham of the great totem of English sport, Dr W.G. Grace.

In the provision of public parks, several of which were created at this time, often from the gardens of large houses, the local authorities were supported, if not propelled, by a great weight of popular opinion. Public libraries were a different matter, and it proved very hard to persuade the ratepayers of Lewisham to support even the most limited scheme. They finally agreed to finance one library, but the funds were so exiguous that the Perry Hill branch opened in 1891 in an unsuitable building and with few books. It was only between 1900 and 1910, with a great deal of help from Andrew Carnegie, that Lewisham established a respectable library service.

It was not that the ratepayers were barbarously opposed to all intellectual improvement, but Lewisham *had* been the home of Samuel Smiles, and his self-help principles were firmly held by many of his late neighbours. Cultural life was to be the product of spontaneous enthusiasm rather than of public provision. In 1900 there were nearly as many literary, musical, and artistic societies in Lewisham as there were sports clubs, and this was the golden age of amateur dramatics. The town's dominant middle classes were a natural recruiting ground for treasurers, secretaries, and every kind of useful committee member, and probably the clubs and societies were the most effective cement in binding the rapidly growing population of Lewisham into a harmonious community.

The Crystal Palace continued, with lessening confidence, to provide for the intellectual stimulation of the distict, but the supreme examples of individual enterprise in this field were the Horniman Museum, and the great arts centre in Blackheath village. Frederick John Horniman, the tea merchant, built the present magnificent museum between 1897 and 1901, and subsequently gave it to the public. In the days before television, and before personal travel was widely possible, Horniman's had an important role in introducing generations of South Londoners to the wonders of the external world. The wonders of the internal world could be explored at the Blackheath Concert Halls, the Conservatoire of Music, and the School of Art, which were built in 1895–6. There were other public halls in the district, and other academies of painting and music, but it was here in Blackheath that the highest standard of teaching first became locally available.

Nevertheless, Booth remarked at the beginning of the new century that 'the district is exceptionally dull so far as public entertainment is concerned' (source 11: VI 159). This was certainly true of amusements likely to have a wide appeal, but things were about to change dramatically. Primitive film shows had been held sporadically in Lewisham since 1896, conducted by philanthropic lecturers or opportunistic showmen in various halls and shops, but it was not until 1909 that the town's first cinema opened for business. It was the Electric Picture Palace in Sangley Road. Thirteen others had followed by 1914, a few in converted shops, but the majority in imposing new buildings that quickly came to dominate most of the shopping centres. Even harder to miss was the Lewisham Hippodrome in Rushey Green, the largest music hall in London, which opened in 1911. As well as featuring all the great names of variety, the Hippodrome gave Lewisham its first taste of professional theatre, and even provided the occasional season of opera.

Formal education in Lewisham was – as usual – a battleground at the end of the nineteenth century. The legislation of 1870 had made elementary education compulsory, and in the capital had placed on the School Board for London the responsibility for providing it where private bodies could not establish sufficient places. Many people in conservative areas like Lewisham were anxious to avoid the plebeian (and, they suspected, pagan) presence of Board schools. The various religious denominations set to work to provide enough extra church schools to satisfy the government, but the rate of population growth overwhelmed their efforts. The non-conformists were least opposed to the government's plans for neutral religious instruction, and the local British and Methodist schools were transferred to the Board during the 1870s. The Anglicans and Roman Catholics put up a much stouter resistance, and their schools still remain today in very respectable numbers. As a result the Board's local activities were mostly restricted during the '70s to enlarging transferred schools and providing temporary accommodation in areas of special need. It was only during the 1880s that many of the Board's own unmistakable schools, Conan Doyle's 'beacons of the future', began to shine in Lewisham, towering over the working class streets in which they were nearly always built. But even the School Board, with its great resources, was always panting desperately in the wake of Lewisham's steeply rising population.

Secondary education, for which an increasing number of scholarships was available, was still the province of the endowed schools. The reforming zeal of the Charity Commissioners resulted in the foundation of several new ones during this period. St Dunstan's College was opened in 1888, and the Lewisham Grammar School for Girls (Prendergast's) in 1890; and Colfe's was rebuilt on its old site in 1889. Private enterprise also played its part. The Girls' Public Day School Company opened two of its fine establishments in Lewisham: one at Blackheath in 1880, the other at Sydenham in

Dunstan's College in 1888.
nard Shaw was soon urging
iend to send his son to 'the
t engineering school in the
rld for boys up to 17 or
reabouts . . . The fee is £12
ear; but they spend three
es that sum on every boy
of their endowments. 200
300 boys there, easy to get
y simply applying,
roughly up to date . . . Of
rse they do not confine
mselves to engineering; but
t is their strong point . . .
d if the distance is a
iculty, move to Lewisham
Lee or thereabouts: it's just
pretty as Ealing & probably
aper' (source 98: p. 560).

1887. Towards the end of its existence the London School Board began to stretch its legal powers by building higher grade schools – Brownhill Road (1903) was the local example – but it was only after the London County Council took control of education in 1904 that state secondary schools began to spread across Lewisham.

In spite of the exhausting education battle, the local churches still found the energy and the money for expansion. The Anglicans, under the inspirational leadership of Augustus Legge, until his promotion to the see of Lichfield, carried through an ambitious programme that produced six new parish churches. The Baptists, Congregationalists, Methodists, and other protestant Churches also moved into the new districts, but the most active builders, after the Anglicans, were the Roman Catholics, who founded four new churches between 1899 and 1909. They were also architecturally assertive, with St Saviour's in the High Street and St William of York in Brockley Park being especially lavish creations.

With the churches and cinemas providing such enticing dispensaries for the opium and pep pills of the people, it was evidently time for those other claimants to popular favour, the pubs and shops, to modernize themselves. Between 1880 and 1914 nearly all the old public houses in Lewisham were rebuilt, most of them in a style of monstrous vulgarity. Even when the results were satisfactory, as in the case of the Black Horse at Rushey Green, most people of taste would readily exchange the showy splendour of the new building for the quiet dignity of the old.

This was also the period when the growth of shops into

Competitive rebuilding was particularly foolish in the cas of old inns which were popul entirely on account of their quaintness. The Brockley Jac (seen here in the 1890s) was favourite haunt of Londoners search of the picturesque. The owners noted the crowds, reb on a lavish scale in 1898, and were left with a pub of interes only to the thirsty locals.

department stores became the dominant trend in retailing. In every shopping centre, drapers who hoped to survive found it necessary to expand, and competition between these embryonic department stores grew fierce. In Lewisham High Street Chiesman, Stroud, Collingwood and Dubois were the leading men, and at Sydenham the dominance of Walter Cobb helped to shift the attention of shoppers from the old High Street at the junction of Dartmouth Road and Kirkdale to the modern retailing centre in Sydenham Road.

1900, when the borough council took over. Having a name to make he naturally pursued a forward policy and was ready to borrow heavily to finance new parks and public buildings. The celebrity he quickly won brought him the personal reward of a rich wife and sister-in-law, both of whose fortunes he used to acquire a group of local newspapers. These were pressed into service to publicize Williams's activities on various local bodies, which grew in time to include the Metropolitan Board of Works and its successor, the London County Council.

In 1900 the new Lewisham Metropolitan Borough Council took over the duties of the Board of Works, and of the commissioners for libraries, baths and cemetaries, and with new responsibilities and powers became the undisputed centre of local government, even though the Guardians of the Poor continued to administer the primitive social services of the day until 1930, when the London County Council took them over. Penge was lost from the district formerly administered by the Board of Works, but it was more than made up for by the addition of the old parish of Lee. This might be regarded as belated revenge for the attempted annexation of Lewisham by Lee in the twelfth century, but it involved little difficulty or unfairness as the two parishes were similar in history and social composition.

Theophilus Williams, now virtual dictator of Lewisham, was mayor of the new borough for the first two years, but then a split in his own party, the Moderates or Conservatives, led to his downfall. In the 1890s he had boasted two addresses, but that was not enough to inspire confidence. Rumours began to circulate that his business empire was supported by a system of fraud and embezzlement, and after his loss of the mayoralty, creditors closed in. The climax came in 1908 with a string of aliases, an attempted escape to France, a dramatic arrest, and a night in Brixton Gaol. A series of sensational court appearances followed, and finally death by an overdose of morphia. These events seem to have established a hearty distrust of flamboyance. For decades, Williams's successors as mayor were the most solidly respectable tradesmen, and it was a long time before the people of Lewisham would again trust the young and ambitious.

Not that the Board of Works or the council had effective control over the town's destiny in the most important matters. Time and again they tried to use their powers in a conservative way, to prevent or delay unwelcome changes in the district. In nearly every instance, national or metropolitan authorities were able to overrule them, in the name of the greater good of the country or the capital. The Board of Works opposed the siting of a fever hospital at Hither Green by the Metropolitan Asylums Board, and a workhouse at Ladywell by the Bermondsey Union, projects not even pretended to be for the benefit of Lewisham. The Prince of Wales came in 1897 and 1900 to open these huge buildings, which certainly altered the destiny of the two villages concerned. Equally ineffectual was the board's attempt to exclude trams, which were to have a vital role in transforming the social composition of the town. Later the borough council experienced the same rebuff when it tried to prevent the building of the huge housing estate at Downham.

If the people of Lewisham were willing to experiment with a new man like Theophilus Williams in local affairs, when it came to national politics their instincts were far more traditional, even atavistic. The town became a parliamentary borough in 1885 and elected as its first MP Lord Lewisham, later sixth Earl of Dartmouth. He secured 4,244 votes against 3,019 for the Radical candidate, Benjamin Whitworth, a Home Ruler who had eccentrically decided to retire as member for Drogheda in order to contest Lewisham.

This long election campaign led to the foundation of a great many political clubs in Lewisham, several of which found excellent premises in the large houses then languishing on the market. An interesting example is the Catford Conservative Working Men's Club, which was opened by Lord Lewisham in 1884 in the building that is now no. 26 Catford Broadway. It was soon found that the name, chosen for solid political reasons, was hampering recruitment among the middle classes, and their wealth was now needed to finance a move to larger premises. In 1885, therefore, the Catford Conservative Club took up residence at its present home, the eighteenth-century farmhouse known as Elmwood.

Elmwood is one Lewisham house that has survived, but at the end of the nineteenth century it must have seemed as if every graceful reminder of Lewisham's past was doomed to the demolition squads. In the High Street and Rushey Green alone the 1880s and '90s saw the loss of Rosenthal and the Maples, Cliff Villa, Lewisham House and the Limes. The houses that escaped total destruction were cobbled into shops. The natural result was a great burgeoning of interest in local history, which led to the formation of the Lewisham Antiquarian Society in 1885. Its leading figure was Leland Lewis Duncan, an outstanding historical writer whose works have proved an inexhaustible quarry for all subsequent students of the subject.

This surge of historical interest mainly expressed itself through the study of the records of the past. Little could be done to stem the destruction of its architectural remains. In 1905, however, public opinion was mobilized to prevent the loss of Colfe's almshouses, which were badly decayed and had been condemned as insanitary. There was a public inquiry and the sum needed to save the buildings was quickly subscribed. It is in shabby contrast that after the

e of the popular picturesque
jects in Southend village
s the Upper Mill, drawn
e in about 1914 by R.C.
rter. By the time it was
versally known as Perry's
m. The mill, and the
ler's house (minus its
nsard roof), survived until
late 1960s as the premises
a timber merchant.

almshouses were damaged during the Second World War the negligence of the council led to their demolition in 1958.

As the First World War approached, Lewisham's population rushed on towards 150,000. In 1911 the figure was 140,470. It was time for the last agricultural area to be overwhelmed, and only the coming of the war delayed its fate. A telling blow was struck before the guns began to roar, when tram services (electrified since 1907) were extended to Southend in 1914. The last village in Lewisham became a playground for the urban population of the rest of the borough. The lower mill pond was turned into a boating lake for children, and the farming activities of the area came more and more to resemble performance art, as the excursionists, armed with camera and sketch pad, began to outnumber the agricultural labourers. It was too much for Lord Forster, Lewisham's principal landowner, who decided to abandon his ancestral home. Southend Hall was soon taken over by a film company as a studio. As Walter Besant had said of South London generally a few years before, 'Alas! the first families are gone: there is now no aristocracy of the suburb left' (source 7: p. 316).

The year 1914 did not need to be made memorable, but even before the war began it had become a signal date in the history of Lewisham. For many hundreds of years the country gentlemen had ruled the parish. In the nineteenth century their power had decayed. Now, finally, the last had departed.

CHAPTER SEVEN

New Estates for Old (1914–1965)

Who could wish to linger over the twentieth century? It is a kindness to abbreviate a catalogue of disasters.

Bombing during the First World War had a negligible impact on Lewisham when compared with the Second, but the moral effects of the conflict proved to have consequences fully as momentous. In 1914 Lewisham was a youthful community. The typical residents were young couples who had recently moved to the big new estates at Catford and Hither Green. The recruiting drive so enthusiastically organized by the council produced a large crop of volunteers, who were quickly transformed into a long return of casualties. Those who came home to Lewisham and the other districts of London in 1918 were the agents of a profound change. The town had been greatly altered during the previous century by evolutionary forces, but now, for the first time, its character was to be seriously affected by political policy. To maintain the war, the government had promised the ordinary soldiers and sailors that they would return to a better life. In particular, they pledged themselves to provide 'homes fit for heroes', but they looked to the local councils to honour the pledge. Legislation had long existed allowing authorities to build houses for the poor, but in a rich and conservative town like Lewisham the idea had never been seriously considered. Now, in November 1918, the Local Government Board wrote to ask what the council was doing to provide housing for demobilized servicemen.

There was undoubtedly a housing shortage, largely caused by the negligible amount of building that had been possible during the previous four years. But in view of the minimal bomb damage and the huge scale of casualties in the war, the majority of the demand must have been political. If the returning servicemen had been prepared to accept the standard of housing they and their parents had been used to before the war, there must have been nearly enough to go round; but government promises had raised expectations, and the organizations of veterans made it vociferously clear that their members required something better. 'The housing of the working classes' became the shibboleth of the 1920s, the test of political correctness.

In this climate Lewisham Council readily agreed to build Lewisham's first council estate, on nine acres of allotments to the east of the High Street. When the gardeners objected, the Lewisham branch of the Comrades of the Great War told the council that:

> the cultivation of nine acres of land within the London area is of no account compared with the necessity of comfortably housing the men that have experienced all the hardships in fighting for their country, not to mention that particular nine acres (source 71: 1919/20, p. 219).

The scheme went ahead in 1920, and by 1921 the first of the eighty-six cottages in Romborough Way and its offshoots were ready. The tenants were almost all local, the majority from Catford.

In the first rush of patriotic enthusiasm the council also raised no objection to the London County Council's plan for a housing estate at Bellingham, even though it was intended principally for the rehousing of families from the inner London boroughs. The breaking point came early in 1920. In 1919 Lewisham had been approached by Deptford and Bermondsey Councils with the idea of a garden city to be built jointly by the three boroughs between Southend and Grove Park. In January 1920 the council debated the question before a noisy public gallery. This was the first Lewisham council to contain any but Municipal Reform (Conservative) members. The Labour Party had eight councillors, and they were among the chief speakers in favour of the new estate. Nervous Municipal Reformers also had reason to support it, for only a week before Labour had captured a Sydenham ward in a by-election. The victor supported 'the full Labour programme, a bold housing policy, and tramway extensions'. Nevertheless the meeting was swayed by an adverse report from the finance committee, and by such arguments as this from Councillor Dodd:

> They were asking in this scheme for the community to pay £1 a week on somebody else's rent. The priveleged gentlemen living in these houses would have more than half their rent paid for them. They must, sooner or later, get back to economic principles, but here they were asking for a socialistic state of things. (Hear, hear.) If a man's house rent were paid by others, it was reasonable to argue that he should have his meat and bread free. (Laughter) (Source 66: 11 February 1920)

After two and a half hours of debate the council resolved by twenty-one votes to nineteen not to accept the scheme, a decision for which they were commended by the Lewisham branch of the Middle Class Union, and condemned by the United Vehicle Workers. Any self-congratulation was brief, however, for the Deptford and Bermondsey authorities had run straight to the London County Council, which announced two months later that it would compulsorily purchase the land in question (plus 150 extra acres adjoining) to build the huge estate now known as Downham.

The result of Lewisham Council's refusal to participate in the scheme was thus an even larger estate, and the loss of control over its design and the selection of the tenants. Financial constraints delayed work, but between 1924 and 1930 the London County Council built seven thousand houses at Downham and added forty thousand to Lewisham's population, quite apart from those contributed by the smaller Bellingham estate, which was largely built between 1920 and 1923. The majority of these new residents were from Deptford, Bermondsey and other inner suburbs. The sudden introduction of these thousands of working people (by the will of an exterior authority) decisively altered the social and political balance of the borough. Although the national trends of the 1930s kept the Conservatives in control of the council and of the two parliamentary seats – Lewisham had been awarded a second in 1918 – the conditions had been created that would enable Labour to sweep them all in 1945. Which makes it all the odder that in 1925, when the party's fortunes were at a low ebb, the only Labour member of the council, Alderman Matthews, should have complained that 'Downham was not for Lewisham; Bellingham was not for Lewisham; they were both ostensibly [*sic*] for the inner boroughs of London – Bermondsey, Rotherhithe, etc.' (source 60: 27 February 1925).

The new estates helped to keep the population of the old parish of Lewisham rushing higher. In 1911 the total had been 140,470; in 1921 it was 152,080. By 1931 the new estates had pushed it to about 192,000, and in 1939 it must have reached its all-time peak of over 200,000. Between the wars Lewisham and Lee were the only parts of the London County Council area to record a significant increase.

During the 1920s and '30s Lewisham proper tried to ignore Downham and Bellingham, perhaps subliminally hoping that they would go away. If the eyes were carefully averted from the south it was still just possible to see Lewisham as the same solid middle class town it had been before the war. As William Pett Ridge, the novelist (who was born in New Cross), remarked in 1927:

> in the direction of Catford and Bromley are extensive estates with houses of quite alarming newness; you turn your back for a moment and find that a park has been seized, old trees rooted up, and hundreds of little dwellings set there.

With this unfortunate exception, Pett Ridge found that the people of

Lewisham formed a vertebra or two of the backbone of the nation, and if that meant they were also a little Pooterish, it could not be helped:

> In Lewisham there is about the houses a certain decorum of age; the gardens are of the handy extent that avoid the help of a paid man. I imagine the houses date from the Sixties, and I know they are occupied by folk engaged in the City, and catching the eight forty-four (or thereabouts) to Cannon Street; there can be seen any week-day morning some fine examples of sprinting that comes from practice in early years with the Blackheath Harriers . . . In the up trains of a morning, and the down trains of an evening, it is possible to hear good conversation on banking, insurance, underwriting, and other activities; when larger and remoter questions are tackled the value is diminished (source 4).

The descriptions of ordinary citizens, though far less rose-tinted, speak of solid contentment. The account of a railwayman, who apparently lived in Mount Ash Road, Sydenham, during the 1930s, reads almost like a Fabian fantasy. He was a loyal union man, an active member of the local Labour Party, and a keen student of the works of Bernard Shaw, Arnold Bennett and H.G. Wells, who might have chronicled his history. He possessed a wireless and gramophone, was fond of gardening, and was especially devoted to rambling in the Kent countryside. 'Even our own locality has a charm for the rambler, and we ofttimes take the dog on a four- or five-hour walk.' The most surprising aspect of this working man's life was that he took his holidays on the continent each year, 'especially in Belgium and Holland'. He particularly relished 'the opportunity of gaining the knowledge, understanding and friendship of our foreign neighbours' (source 100: IX 402–6).

In 1932 the *New Survey of London Life and Labour* gave a more scientific, but not at all contradictory, report on Lewisham:

> The borough is essentially a residential suburb of London and is largely of middle-class character, though the inhabitants vary from wealthy upper middle class to working class, according, as a rule, to the elevation of the land on which the houses stand and to the degree of proximity of open spaces . . . There are practically no slums in the borough, but . . . Railway Terrace, Ladywell, and part of the Bell Green area in Lower Sydenham near the gasworks almost deserve the name . . . Lewisham contains a good many large houses originally built for well-to-do families, but situated in neighbourhoods from which such families have withdrawn. The Borough Council have converted a number of such houses into flats . . . Germans form the majority of foreign-born inhabitants – Sydenham has long been a favourite place of residence for German business people in London. There are only 4.8 per cent. of the inhabitants of Lewisham living in poverty, the lowest proportion for any of the boroughs in the

Eastern Area. The percentage of persons in middle-class circumstances (30.8) is higher than in any other borough . . . (source 100: III 381).

Despite this finding that Lewisham contained practically no slums, the late 1930s was a period of active 'slum clearance' in the town. This is an illustration of the way in which good ideas can go sour when they pass from the hands of their imaginative originators into those of dull bureaucrats. Once the mechanism is in place it will find work to do, needed or not. Some of the courts and alleyways swept away at this time were certainly ones of which any town could be glad to be rid, but many were cottages that could easily have been improved to modern standards, and would now be regarded as highly desirable. The *New Survey* also noted that 44,000 of the 78,000 occupied persons living in Lewisham worked outside the borough, half of them in the City or in Westminster, and that a large proportion of them were clerks. The natural habitat of the clerk is the semi-detached house, so in order to provide more of them nearly all of Lewisham's surviving old mansions and villas were demolished between the wars. Few of them had been houses in their last years: some were clubs, some schools, some hotels.

The gentlemen's houses had once been the first feature noticed by visitors to Lewisham, but now it was the shops, cinemas and public buildings. Lewisham was the leading shopping centre for miles around. Proud residents boasted that 'you can get all you want within a hop, skip, and a jump of the Obelisk!' (source 4).

Electricity for domestic use became locally available in the 1890s and was first suggested for street lighting in 1893. An experimental lamp was erected at the corner of Bromley Road and Arran Road in 1910, and others were installed privately in the main shopping parades. But conservative Lewisham declined to introduce a general scheme until 1933, and the last conversions were made in, of all unlikely years, 1940, with the result that some streets did not see the light until the return of peace.

The monster that was to wreak more havoc in Lewisham than the Luftwaffe was still a favourite pet between the wars, but even then the motor car was flexing its muscles. All over the town, houses and shops were giving way to garages and filling stations, and the first dual carriageways were slicing through the remaining pockets of countryside. The demolition of Southend Hall was decreed so that Whitefoot Lane could be transformed from Lewisham's most celebrated beauty spot into one of its leading eyesores. The sad conclusion is that even if the Second World War had never occurred, the ruin of Lewisham, though it would obviously have been retarded, might not ultimately have been much less complete.

One country house which retained its true character u the end was Brockley Hall. The old farmhouse on this s was rebuilt in the 1790s, as seen in this drawing of abou 1860. The estate then belonged to the Noakes family, Bermondsey brewer The last of the line was the eccentric Maude Noakes, w kept a menagerie of pets, an used to bury them all over t extensive grounds. She kep the impatient builders waiti for her death until 1931, bu year later Brockley Hall Ro was constructed on the site the old house.

s the old mansions of the
ealthy tumbled, in 1932
ere arose symbolically the
aumont Palace, one of the
est specimens from that
ost luxurious era of cinema
ilding. This is the
ditorium, sketched by the
chitect W.E. Trent, or one of
s staff. It might have seemed
gnificant that Bellingham
rm was demolished in
32, but it is curious to note
at the little wooden
rmhouse had stood for two
ndred and fifty years, while
e gigantic and triumphant
aumont was destined to last
r only sixty.

This is no small claim, because the damage to the town during the war was immense. In the borough as a whole (including the parish of Lee) over a thousand civilians were killed by bombing, and many more were injured or made homeless. Some 3,600 houses were destroyed, 15,550 were seriously damaged, and only 370 escaped entirely unharmed. Fate maliciously picked out some of the best surviving buildings for destruction or terminal damage – Colfe's almshouses and school, Holly Hedge House, Park House at Southend – while carefully shielding Selwyn Court, the blot on Blackheath village.

At the end of the war Lewisham was littered with derelict buildings and bomb sites. In other circumstances it would have been possible to restore the one and to use the other for sympathetic infilling. But in 1945 the mood of the country, accurately reflected in Lewisham, favoured quick and drastic solutions to every problem, and the Labour Party was called in to supply them. It set about the rebuilding of the town with vigour, but with little tact or imagination. Many damaged properties were unnecessarily destroyed, and the loss of the odd house in a road or terrace was all too readily taken as an excuse for blanket demolition, with compulsory purchase powers widely used. The spirit of class warfare in which the work was sometimes approached is suggested by a speech made in 1951 (when the Conservatives were back in control of Lewisham Council) by Fred Copeman, OBE, who had been chairman of the Housing Committee between 1945 and 1949.

> He accused the Conservative members of the council of opposing a scheme that would transfer a mass of people into an exclusive residential area of Sydenham, which normally catered for a privileged section of the community, and said, 'It's the same with the generals and the admirals who live at Blackheath, where there was trouble with the Georgian Society. You can tell their outlook. They objected because it would change the Georgian architecture. So we said, "All right, brother", and we produced a block of flats in Georgian architecture.' (source 60: 19 October 1951)

Blocks of flats were almost universal in the new council estates. This was partly the result of post-war poverty, but the decline from the garden city ideal of public housing had begun in the late 1920s. The first Lewisham estate at Romborough Way, and the great London County Council developments at Bellingham and Downham had consisted of cottages, monotonous in the mass, but well built, thoroughly appreciated by their tenants, and still perfectly efficient homes. But the Lewisham and London County Councils were turning increasingly to the – in the short term – cheaper alternative. In the part of Bellingham beyond Southend Lane, built in the late 1930s, sixty per cent of the dwellings were provided in flats. On the Honor

The Hether Grove estate took the place of Camps Hill House, which had been built in 1824 by Henry Lee, the Loampit Hill brickmaker. It was later the home of a managing director of the P& Line. This view of the garden front is from an 1879 sale catalogue.

Oak estate (built throughout the '30s, partly in Deptford) only flats appeared, and in blocks of a peculiarly ugly and barrack-like design.

After the war the blocks became bigger and nastier still. The use of cheap methods and materials proved to be a poor economy, for the two largest post-war estates lasted only forty years before they had to be largely rebuilt. These were the Flower House and Hether Grove estates at Southend and Hither Green, which replaced large houses that had fallen derelict after bomb damage.

When the Conservative councils that ran Lewisham between 1949 and 1956 showed less enthusiasm for grand housing schemes, the London County Council again intervened in the borough's affairs to make a compulsory purchase order for St Mary's, Sydenham Hill. This fine house, designed by Frederick Faber himself in 1852 as a country retreat for the fathers of Brompton Oratory, had a garden that was one of the treasures – one of the few treasures – of Lewisham. The fathers were unceremoniously ejected and the Sydenham Hill estate was built, as if expressly to prove how little it is possible to make even of the most magnificent site.

The 1960s were gloomy years of industrial decay, closures, and demolitions. Many of the institutions created during the expansive late Victorian and Edwardian period now withered and died. Sporting, social and artistic clubs gave up the struggle for existence. The department stores declined until only two precariously survived. Most of the cinemas closed, and were either demolished or converted to some ignominious use. The ranks of the churches continued to thin, and the small number of old houses was reduced still further by the destruction of Riverdale in 1962, Camden House and the

Chestnuts in 1963, and Round Hill House and the Orchard in 1964.

In replacement, that ugly decade offered an array of brutalist buildings, which had only the merit of aiding the suicidal tendencies they seemed designed to inspire. Some characteristic monuments of the 1960s in the High Street and Rushey Green are Eros House, Capital House and Rosenthal House, the Lewisham Park tower blocks, and a telephone exchange of breathtaking banality.

The intensive building of the 1940s and '50s did not entirely succeed in reversing the fall in population that the town had experienced as a result of the war. It is probable that by 1939 the total for the old parish of Lewisham had passed 200,000. In 1951, after the building of the Hether Grove and Flower House estates and many smaller schemes, the census figure was about 196,000, only four thousand more than in 1931. It might have been expected that as the bomb sites continued to be recolonized, as large Victorian houses were demolished or converted into flats, and as more and more back development was permitted on the formerly ample gardens of Lewisham, the population would have regained its pre-war level. In fact it was scarcely changed at about 196,000 in 1961, and thereafter was to fall: to about 179,000 in 1971, 155,000 in 1981, and 153,000 in 1991. This was in line with the general trend in London, reflecting the continued flight of the better off from the city, now to the Home Counties. In fact the same centrifugal force that had made Lewisham grow was now making it shrink. This loss of residents had political consequences. For the 1950 general election Lewisham had been redistributed into three constituencies: South, which was safe for Labour, and West and North, both Conservative marginals. In 1974 the evidence of falling population was to lead to the constituencies being cut back to the current East and West Lewisham.

As a result of the continuing drift of the middle classes away from the town, Labour regained control of the council in 1956, and held it until the abolition of the metropolitan boroughs in 1965. This was despite the Conservatives winning the 1959 election, when creative use of the retiring aldermen and the mayor's casting vote enabled Labour to conjure up a majority. A.P. Herbert commemorated this in some verses entitled *Lewishame*, ending:

> Henceforth, whenever grabbing wins the day
> And trickery defies the People's writ,
> 'You've done a Lewisham,' the world will say,
> 'You've done a Lewisham' – and all will spit.

(source 22)

Such disputes became irrelevant in 1965, when Lewisham was combined with Deptford to form the new London borough. Permanent one-party rule is as unhealthy for a town as it is for a country, and constant fluctuations of leadership are not much better. The situation in Lewisham during the two post-war decades approached the ideal, with a single party generally in control, but with a dissatisfied electorate able to remove it without a psephological earthquake. Deptford, though, had long been a Labour stronghold, and its fusion now made Lewisham the same. The last election under the old borough structure had produced 28 Labour councillors and 27 Conservatives. The strengths on the new council were 45 to 15. These members were elected in 1964, Labour's year nationally, but even in the Conservative's best subsequent periods Labour has never been in any danger of losing control of Lewisham's local government. That old Lewisham continues to be marginal is shown by the fluctuating fortunes of the parties in its two parliamentary constituencies.

The amalgamation with Deptford marked an epoch in the history of Lewisham. The absorption of Lee in 1900 had been of minor significance because the two parishes had been so similar, but Deptford and Lewisham had little in common, socially or historically. There was no reason for them to be combined except the statistical convenience of the commissioners who planned the new structure of London government. The result was that from 1964 the voting of Deptford determined the balance of power in Lewisham, and its poverty set the political agenda, for by nearly every criterion the five Deptford wards are the poorest in the modern borough. The situation might be compared to the union of East and West Germany, but without any emotional cement. As so often before, Lewisham suffered because it could not control its own destiny, but was made the vehicle of London-wide social engineering. There is a case for saying that the independent existence of Lewisham ended in 1965. The London borough still bears its name, but the problems that dominate its politics are the problems of Deptford.

Around Lewisham

The principal object of this tour is to discover buildings, and the sites of buildings, mentioned in the history, or associated with events described there. Throughout this tour instructions about the route are given in bold type.

The walk begins in Lewisham High Street, at St Mary's, the ancient parish church of the village.

It is worth examining the tower of St Mary's church. The lower portion is the oldest structure in Lewisham, and the only surviving fragment of the medieval building. The interior should be visited if the church is open, especially for the sake of its fine monuments, and there are also some very interesting tombs in the churchyard. On the opposite side of the road from the church are the St Mary's National Schools, the original block of 1833 to the south (right) and the extension dated 1860 to the north. Next to it is the entrance to Romborough Way, the principal road of Lewisham's first council estate, built in the early 1920s.

Proceed to the corner of Ladywell Road, noting the following buildings on the opposite side of the High Street.

The little shops at the corner of Legge Street (nos 315–19) occupy the front garden of a house built late in the seventeenth or early in the eighteenth century, and thus one of the oldest surviving in Lewisham. Nos 299 and 301, now part of Olby's premises, are the last remaining examples of a style of house once common in the High Street. They were built in 1791. Next to them is Streete House (now, much altered, the Hire Shop), which was once the home of Joshua Morton, and afterwards of Methusalem Davies.

Pause to compare the view northwards with the one in the 1857 painting. Then cross Ladywell Road at the traffic lights to Ladywell House.

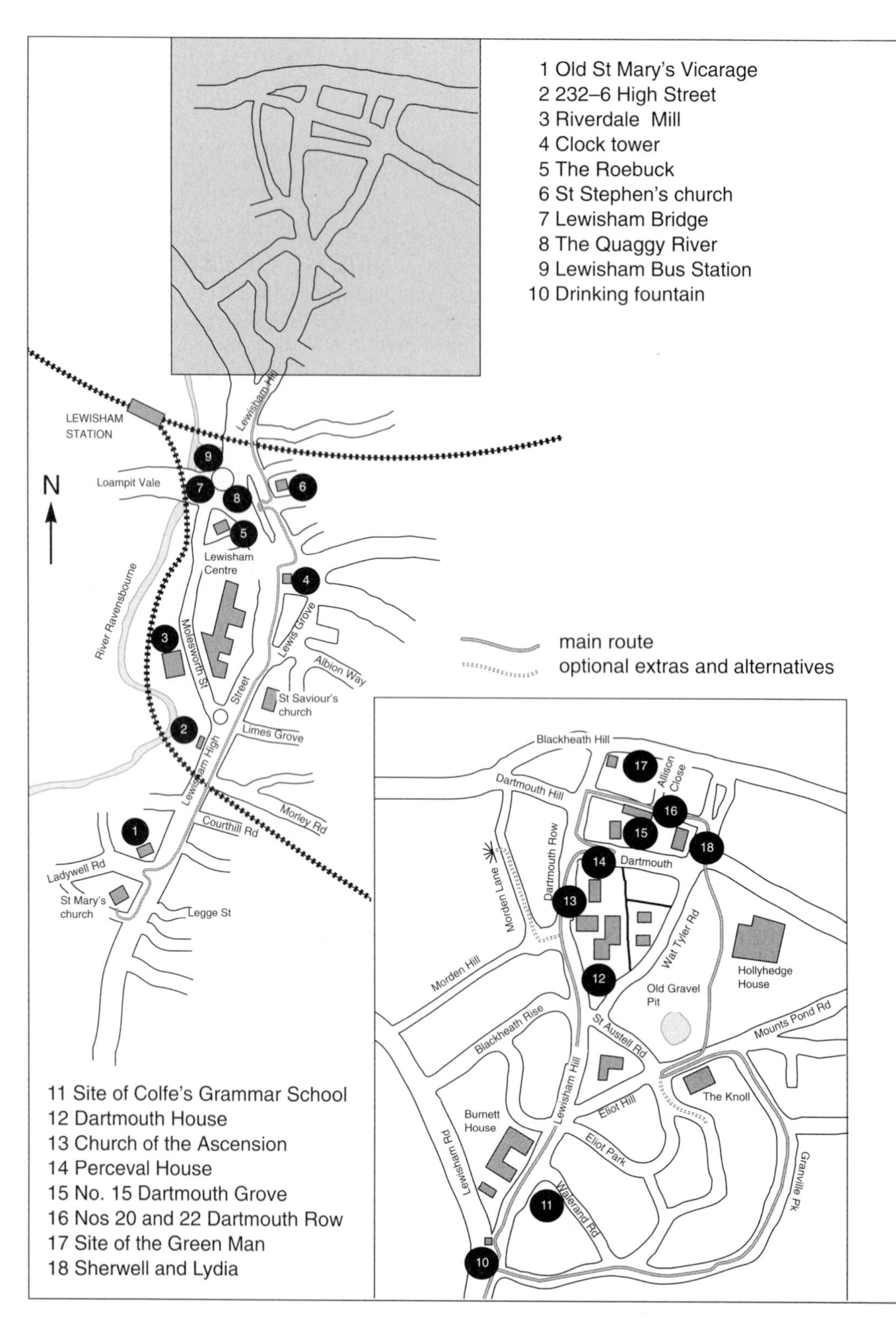
1 Old St Mary's Vicarage
2 232–6 High Street
3 Riverdale Mill
4 Clock tower
5 The Roebuck
6 St Stephen's church
7 Lewisham Bridge
8 The Quaggy River
9 Lewisham Bus Station
10 Drinking fountain
LEWISHAM STATION
Loampit Vale
Lewisham Hill
Lewisham Centre
River Ravensbourne
Molesworth St
Lewis Grove
Albion Way
St Saviour's church
Limes Grove
Lewisham High Street
Morley Rd
Courthill Rd
Ladywell Rd
St Mary's church
Legge St
N
main route
optional extras and alternatives
Blackheath Hill
Dartmouth Hill
Allison Close
Dartmouth Row
Dartmouth
Morden Lane
Wat Tyler Rd
Morden Hill
Hollyhedge House
Old Gravel Pit
Blackheath Rise
St Austell Rd
Mounts Pond Rd
Lewisham Hill
The Knoll
Eliot Hill
Burnett House
Eliot Park
Lewisham Rd
Granville Pk
Walerand Rd
11 Site of Colfe's Grammar School
12 Dartmouth House
13 Church of the Ascension
14 Perceval House
15 No. 15 Dartmouth Grove
16 Nos 20 and 22 Dartmouth Row
17 Site of the Green Man
18 Sherwell and Lydia

This is the former St Mary's vicarage, built by George Stanhope from 1692 to 1693 and visited by Swift in 1711. There have been two extensions to the house, one at the rear between 1879 and 1881, and one to the west (left) built in 1894–5.

At the traffic lights cross the High Street to the Ladywell Leisure Centre, and walk north to the corner of Courthill Road.

The Lewisham United Reformed church, formerly Congregational, was built in 1866 on the site of the Rookery, the headquarters of the Lewisham Nursery. On the other side of the High Street, on the far corner of Whitburn Road, is a rare survival of a large house from the village's most prosperous period. Brooklands was built in 1782, or just before, on the site of an old tan yard, at a time when Lewisham's industry was in decline.

Cross Courthill Road at the traffic lights and continue up the east side of the High Street to Limes Grove. Between Morley Road and Limes Grove compare the large furniture shop opposite with the houses previously on this site, as shown in the illustration.

he view northwards from e gates of Lewisham ouse, painted by C. Bigot 1857. The turning to adywell Road is on the ft, and the tall house is the resent 328 High Street. st beyond it, with the gn, was the beerhouse alled – earlier at least – the ve Bells. The cottages on e right were at the corner f Hither Green Lane, hich then ran down to the igh Street. Above the epherd's head are the ains of the ancient house alled the Rookery. The ongregational (now United eformed) church was built n the site in 1866.

Opposite Limes Grove is Molesworth Street, which began as a quiet cul-de-sac off Loampit Vale, but which has been destructively promoted to one of the town's major roads. Among the victims of the new roundabout was one of the four villas (built in about 1820) known as Camden Place. The other three precariously survive to the south of Molesworth Street, with their shop-fronts removed. A short way up Molesworth Street on the left, just at the bend, may be seen the Riverdale Mill, the sole survivor of the thirteen mills on the Ravensbourne mentioned in Domesday Book. The present building dates from about 1830.

Proceed to the Roman Catholic church, St Saviour's.

The church itself was built in 1909, the presbytery and campanile in 1929. They stand ecumenically on the site of John Wesley's favourite haunt, the Limes, a house commemorated by a plaque on the first shop past the church.

Continue to the corner of Albion Way.

Ahead on the left is the Lewisham Centre, which opened in 1975, on the site once occupied by Grove House. The shops and banks between Lewis Grove and the High Street stand on what was Watch House Green until the passing of the Lewisham Enclosure Act. There are very few old buildings in this part of the High Street

These two houses, demolishe in about 1878, were replaced by the shops now numbered 232 to 236 High Street, and currently occupied as a singl large furniture store. Henry Wood's sketch (from memor shows the houses as they we in the 1850s. They were sometimes referred to as 5 ar 6 Camden Place, though olde than the other houses in that group, and the one on the lef was additionally called Abinger Cottage. Note the stream in the foreground.

he Lewisham Cage, a
mall octagonal building,
ood on Watch House
reen, close to the stocks
nd whipping post, very
kely on the spot now
ccupied by the post office.
was used for the
mporary imprisonment of
etty offenders, at least until
ie day when some
nfortunates set fire to their
traw bedding, and were
urnt to death before the
ey could be found.

because of the high value of the land, and because the area was devastated by a flying bomb in 1944.

Continue up the High Street to the clock tower, which has an inscription explaining its origin. Then cross to Tower House, which stands on the High Pavement, and continue to the footbridge over the River Quaggy in front of St Stephen's, noting in passing the modern Roebuck in Rennell Street.

From here there is a good view across the new roundabout to the modern Lewisham Bridge, which could scarcely be less like the old one sketched by Henry Wood. St Stephen's has only the base of a tower because the river bank would not bear the weight of the one that was intended by the architect, Sir George Gilbert Scott.

Walk north under the railway bridge, continue to the foot of Lewisham Hill, and cross to the obelisk that stands at its junction with Lewisham Road.

This obelisk, a disused drinking fountain, is of thoroughly mysterious origin. It appears to have been erected in the late 1860s or early '70s, at the time when there was considerable building on Lewisham Hill, and the obelisk may have had some decorative connection with that development. A number of these large Victorian houses survive.

Walk up the western side of Lewisham Hill to a point opposite Walerand Road.

Lacey House and Burnett House, the large blocks of flats on the west side of Lewisham Hill, have taken the place of a handsome row of twenty houses called Dartmouth Terrace, which were built in about 1820. They were badly damaged in 1944 by the flying bomb that destroyed Colfe's Grammar School. The site of Colfe's from 1652 until 1964 was at the southern corner of Walerand Road. The wall and gates of the second school (opened in 1890) survive in Walerand Road, having been retained for the flats now on the site.

Resume the climb until opposite Eliot Park.

THE ROEBUCK
NICHOLL'S ALES
The ROE BUCK

pposite: The Roebuck was
e of the leading inns in
e village during the
ghteenth and nineteenth
nturies, but its
mmanding site at the
rner of the High Street
d Loampit Vale
entually proved its
doing. The value of the
nd was too great a
mptation to the owners,
d shortly after the date of
is painting (1885), the pub
as rebuilt on the site of the
tle building on the left, at
e corner of Rennell Street.
e third and present
ebuck is in Rennell Street
elf.
low: The medieval stone
idge at Lewisham was
built in brick in the
cond half of the
ghteenth century. Henry
ood's sketch from
emory shows it as it was
the 1850s, viewed from
south. This in turn was
placed in 1872–3 by the
n bridge which survived
til 1993.

Note the attractive nos 1 to 6 Eliot Hill, opposite, which were built in 1864. The especially fine corner pair were designed to give the impression of a single detached house.

Proceed to the corner of Blackheath Rise.

The last three Victorian survivors in Lewisham Hill, nos 59, 61 and 63, were built in 1865. The restrained dignity of their design has made the original name of no. 63 – Hollywood – no longer appropriate. These surviving houses and their lost companions were known as Dartmouth Point, which had been the name of this corner long before.

Continue as far as Morden Hill.

This is the entrance to Dartmouth Row, the best street in Lewisham. The large, plain mid-eighteenth century building on the opposite side is Dartmouth House, which might have been called the manor house of Lewisham, but never was. That is perhaps because the earls were only occasional residents here, and in the earlier house on the site. Beyond it is the Church of the Ascension, formerly the Dartmouth Chapel, the innocent cause of much dissension. Opposite the chapel stood Dartmouth Hill House, from the garden of which Alderman Macaulay enjoyed such a fine view. Those anxious to see how two hundred years have treated it should take a detour down Morden Hill and along Morden Lane to a vantage point thoughtfully provided for the purpose.

Stroll past the church – Dartmouth Row is strolling territory – and take a stand opposite nos 21 and 23.

This is Perceval House, the best building in the best street, for all that it has been divided into two dwellings for more than a century, and those dwellings into flats for much of that period. Comparison with the 1841 view (on page 33) reveals some alterations, but this is still unmistakably the 1690s mansion. The situation on the other side of the road is a good deal less clear cut. The best group, nos 36a to 28, begins opposite Perceval House. It has many charms, not least that of variety, but these houses have been so often altered, enlarged, and subdivided, that it is very difficult to determine what survives of late seventeenth-century fabric.

Alderman George Macaulay lived at Dartmouth Hill Hous[e] one of the largest of the original Dartmouth Row properties. It was demolishe[d] in 1892, and nos 38 and 40 now occupy the site. This 1790 view from his garden looks towards Plough Garlic[k] or Telegraph Hill. The large white building in the distanc[e] is almost certainly Stone House, the home of George Gibson, the architect of St Mary's.

Cross the road, and turn into Dartmouth Grove to examine no 5.

This is a good house of the late eighteenth century, extended and refaced in the middle of the nineteenth, when it was a school. The land between Dartmouth Grove and Dartmouth Hill was the site of the Blackheath Fair, as attended by John Evelyn in 1683. Lord Dartmouth's highly moral suppression of the fair had the useful by-product of allowing him to begin building on this valuable land. No. 5 was one of the results.

Return to Dartmouth Row, and continue up the east side to the corner of Dartmouth Hill.

Nos 20 and 22 Dartmouth Row are rather smaller than most in the group from 28 to 36a, for this was the less grand end of the street. No. 20 was built early in the nineteenth century, but no. 22 forms substantially the original house of about 1690, although centuries of alteration have obscured the fact.

Turn right into Dartmouth Hill, cross the road and walk to Allison Close, noting the following on the way.

The otherwise uninteresting no. 18 Dartmouth Hill stands on the site of the rebel chapel built by Joshua Morton in about 1790. The strange pair 20 and 22 date from the 1770s. Their position directly on the road was dictated by the shallowness of the site. No. 20 has a blue plaque to James Glaisher, the astronomer. Allison Close, the development of flats to the north, was built in 1972 in place of the Green Man, Lewisham's premier inn, which had its entrance in Blackheath Hill on the other side of the site.

Continue to the end of Dartmouth Hill, where the great prospect of Blackheath itself opens to the view.

Now the peaceful domain of exercise, kite-flying, picnicking, sunbathing, Blackheath has been the scene of countless colourful and dramatic events, royal, military, political and religious. Murder and highway robbery were commonplace until the increase of houses tamed the Heath, and then it became one of the great historic centres of English sport. The two fine houses between Dartmouth Hill and Dartmouth Grove are Sherwell and Lydia, built by the architect Thomas Gayfere in or shortly after 1776. The design had great influence on later Blackheath semi-detached architecture.

Turn south in front of these two houses, pass diagonally over Wat Tyler Road and cut across the Heath to the western side of the Hollyhedge House complex. Follow its boundary fence to the corner, then continue south across the Heath to the old gravel pit, and skirt its eastern edge as far as the road.

·chery was all the rage on ackheath in the 1780s and 0s, when the Duke of ccleuch, Captain General of e Archers, lived at Montagu ouse. This print shows one the grand reviews of the tional Toxophilite Society the 1780s; and the Heath is also the venue for the eetings of its feminine uivalent, the British nazons.

The large house at the corner of St Austell Road is the Knoll, which was built in the late 1790s, probably to the designs of George Gibson. Since about 1905 it has been divided into two dwellings, one of them called the Old Knoll. The most attractive face of the house is the original garden front. It may be admired from Oakcroft Road, which branches from St Austell.

Walk east along Mounts Pond Road to the northern end of Granville Park. It was from this point that the artist of 1857 (see page 61) made his imaginary sketch of the ideal development of the road.

With its many fine semi-detached houses of the 1850s and '60s, Granville Park forms an attractive route of return to Lewisham High Street, the finishing point of this tour. The blue plaque to Samuel Smiles on no. 11 is sadly a blunder. The apostle of self-help really lived from 1860 to 1863 at no. 12, on the opposite side of Granville Park.

Sources

The standard history of Lewisham is Leland Duncan's, first published in 1908. This and his other books have been the foundation of all subsequent writings on the subject. If Duncan's name appears more often in these pages when I have been obliged to disagree with him than when I have borrowed his words or thoughts, it is because that dissent has been so exceptional, and that theft so much a matter of habit. Other sources which have been outstandingly useful for all sections of the book are the revised edition of Hasted's *History of Kent: the Hundred of Blackheath,* edited by Henry Drake; Neil Rhind's various volumes, especially *The Heath;* and L.A.J. Baker's excellent collection of newspaper cuttings. For the medieval period, in which I feel very much a stranger, the work of Jennifer Mills has been invaluable; and for the late Victorian history I have been able to draw heavily on the classic survey of Charles Booth.

The main books and manuscript collections consulted are given below. In the text references the number before the colon identifies a source in this list; and after the colon comes the page or document number.

1. Andrews, D.H.B., *Elementary Education in the Lewisham District, 1870–1903* (thesis, 1965).
2. Bagshaw, Samuel, *History, Gazeteer, and Directory of the County of Kent* (1847)
3. Baker, L.A.J., *Churches in the Hundred of Blackheath* (1961)
4. Baker, L.A.J., collection of newspaper cuttings, Lewisham Local History Centre
5. Beattie, W., *The Life and Letters of Thomas Campbell* (1849)
6. Bellenger, T.J., *Idealism and the Real World . . . : the Downham Estate, 1924–1930* (thesis, 1986)
7. Besant, Walter, *South London* (1899)
8. Black, Alistair, *The Downham Estate, 1924–1939* (thesis 1981, revised edn, 1985)
9. Blackheath Hundred Justices' Minutes (Greenwich Local History Library)

Booth, Charles, *Life and Labour of the People in London* (4th edn, 1902–3):

10. ——, *First Series: Poverty* (first published 1889–91)
11. ——, *Third Series: Religious Influences* (first published 1902)
12. Butler, Samuel, *The Note-Books*, ed. H.F. Jones (1912)
13. Butts, Robert, *Historical Guide to Lewisham, Ladywell, Lee, Blackheath, and Eltham* (1878)
14. Byrne, M. St Clare (ed.), *The Elizabethan Home* (1949 edn)

15. Chalklin, C.W., *Seventeenth-Century Kent* (1965)
16. Chatto and Windus, *The Suburban Homes of London: a Residential Guide* (1881)
17. Cherry, Bridget and Nikolaus Pevsner, *The Buildings of England: London 2, South* (1983)
18. *Clark's Forest Hill and Sydenham Directory* (1858)
19. Cole, Oswald, 'The Quest for Cameron Corbett', *Lewisham Local History Society Transactions* (1973)
20. Colfe MSS., Leathersellers' Company
21. Collier, John Payne, *Memoirs of Edward Alleyn* (1841)
22. *Daily Telegraph*, 21 May 1959
23. Darby, H.C. (ed.), *The Historical Geography of England* (1936)
24. Defoe, Daniel, *A Tour Thro' the Whole Island of Great Britain*, vol. I (1724)
25. Dickens, Charles, *The Letters*, vol. III, ed. M. House et al (1974)
26. Dowson, Ernest, *The Letters*, ed. D. Flower and H. Maas (1967)
27. Doyle, Sir Arthur Conan, *Sherlock Holmes: the Complete Short Stories* (1928)
28. Drake, Henry H. (ed.), *Hasted's History of Kent, Corrected, Enlarged and Continued . . . : part I. The Hundred of Blackheath* (1886)
29. Duncan, Leland L., *A History of Colfe's Grammar School* (1910)
30. Duncan, Leland L., *History of the Borough of Lewisham* (1908)
31. Duncan, Leland L., *Odds and Ends of Lewisham History* (1913)
32. Duncan, Leland L., *The Parish Church of St Mary, Lewisham* (1892)
33. Duncan, Leland L. (ed.), *The Register of Marriages, Christenings and Burials in the Church of Saint Mary, Lewisham* (1891)
34. Dunkin, Alfred John (ed.), *The Archaeological Mine*, vol. I (1855)
35. Edwards, J., *Topographical Surveys from London through . . . Kent* (2nd edn, 1820)
36. Evelyn, John, *The Diary*, ed. E.S. de Beer (1955)
37. Faber, Frederick William, *Faber, Poet and Priest: Selected Letters*, ed. R. Addington (1974)
38. FitzGerald, Edward, *The Letters*, ed. A.M. and A.B. Terhune (1980)
39. Forest Hill Boys' and Girls' Industrial Homes: Annual Reports, 1873–1932
40. George, Ken, *'Two Sixpennies Please': Lewisham's Early Cinemas* (1987)
41. George, Mary Dorothy, *London Life in the Eighteenth Century* (3rd edn, 1951)
42. Glover, Judith, *The Place Names of Kent* (1976)
43. *Greenwich* (later *Greenwich and Lewisham*) *Antiquarian Society, Transactions*, 1905–90
44. Greenwich Local History Library
45. *Greenwich, Woolwich and Deptford Gazette*, 1834–8
46. Greenwood, C., *An Epitome of County History*, vol. I: *Kent* (1838)
47. Harvey, John, *Early Nurserymen* (1974)
48. Hasted, Edward, *The History and Topographical Survey of the County of Kent* (1778-99)

    Hasted, see also Drake

49. Hayward, J.F., *English Cutlery, Sixteenth to Eighteenth Century* (Victoria and Albert Museum, 1956)
50. Historical Manuscripts Commission, *Calendar of the MSS of the Earl of Dartmouth* (1887–96)
51. Historical Manuscripts Commission, *Calendar of the MSS of the Marquess of Salisbury* (1883–1976)
52. Holyband, Claudius, *The French Littelton,* ed. M. St Clare Byrne (1953)
53. Home and Infirmary for Sick Children (later The South-Eastern Hospital for Children): Annual Reports, 1878–1938
54. Hyde, Shirley et al, *The Social Atlas of Poverty in Lewisham* (1989)
55. Jeffery, Tom, *The Politics of National Unity: Parliamentary Elections in Lewisham, 1918–1945* (thesis, *c.* 1978)
56. Jones, Henry Festing, *Samuel Butler: a Memoir* (1919)
57. Judge, Roy, *Hither Green, 1884–1984* (1984)
58. Judge, Roy, 'St Swithun's Parish and Corbett Estate', *Lewisham Local History Society Transactions* (1973)
59. Kent Archive Office
60. *Kentish Mercury,* 1838–1965
61. [Kerr, Father Ralph], 'The Oratory in London', *The Oratory Parish Magazine,* vol. III, nos 11 and 12 (1923)
62. Kirby, Herbert Charles, and Leland L. Duncan, *The Monumental Inscriptions . . . of S. Mary, Lewisham* (1889)
63. Kirby, J.W., 'The Royal Subsidy of 1641 and the Levy of 1644', *Transactions of the Greenwich and Lewisham Antiquarian Society,* vol. VI (1963)
64. Lewisham Board of Works: Annual Reports, 1856–1900
65. Lewisham Board of Works: Minutes, 1874–99
66. *Lewisham Borough News,* 1901–65
67. Lewisham Local History Centre
68. *Lewisham Local History Society Transactions,* 1963–86
69. Lewisham, Metropolitan Borough: Annual Reports, 1900–62
70. Lewisham, Metropolitan Borough: Guides, 1917–60
71. Lewisham, Metropolitan Borough: Minutes, 1900–65
72. London County Council, *London Housing* (1937)
73. Lysons, Daniel, *The Environs of London* (1792–6)
74. Lysons, Daniel, *The Environs of London* (2nd edn, 1811)
75. Macartney, Sylvia and John West, *A History of Lewisham Silk Mills* (1979)
76. Markham, Violet R., *Paxton and the Bachelor Duke* (1935)
77. Marryat, Florence, *The Life and Letters of Frederick Marryat* (1872)
78. Martin, A.R., 'The Alien Priory of Lewisham', *Transactions of the Greenwich and Lewisham Antiquarian Society,* vol. III, no. 3 (1927)
79. Martin, A.R., 'The Old Church of St Mary, Lewisham', *Transactions of the Greenwich and Lewisham Antiquarian Society*, vol. III, no. 2 (1927)
80. Masters, Betty R., 'Some Bridge House Lands South of the Thames,' *Lewisham Local History Society Transactions* (1972)

81. Mills, Jennifer, *The Priory at Lewisham* (thesis, 1986)
82. Murray, John (pub.), *Handbook for Travellers in Kent* (5th edn, 1892)
83. Myers, Sam Price, *London South of the River* (1949)
84. New Cross Turnpike Trust, *A Collection of All the Acts of Parliament relating to the New Cross Turnpike* (1765)
85. Olsen, Donald J., *The Growth of Victorian London* (1976)
86. *Pall Mall Gazette*, 27 September 1875
87. Pepper, Ronald William, *Urban Development of Lewisham* (thesis, 1966)
88. Prockter, Adrian, *Forest Hill and Sydenham* (1987)
89. Prockter, Adrian, *The London and Croydon Railway: 150th Anniversary, 1839–1989* (1989)
90. Public Record Office
91. Raymond, J.G., *The Life of Thomas Dermody* (1806)
92. Rhind, Neil, *Blackheath Village and Environs, 1790–1990,* vol. I: *The Village and Blackheath Vale* (1976, revised edn 1993)
93. Rhind, Neil, *Blackheath Village and Environs, 1790–1970,* vol. II: *Wricklemarsh, the Cator Estate . . .* (1983)
94. Rhind, Neil, *The Heath* (1987)
95. Rogers, Samuel, *Table-Talk,* ed. M. Bishop (1952)
96. St Mary, Lewisham, Parish of: Year Books, 1880–91
97. St Olave and St John, Southwark, *Rental Book of the United Charities* (1893)
98. Shaw, Bernard, *Collected Letters 1874–1897*, ed. Dan H. Lawrence (1965)
99. Smiles, Samuel, *The Autobiography* (1905)
100. Smith, Sir Hubert Llewellyn et al, *The New Survey of London Life and Labour* (1930–5)
101. Stanley, Sir John, *Praeterita* (in *The Early Married Life of Maria Josepha, Lady Stanley*) ed. J.H. Adeane (1899)
102. Swift, Jonathan, *The Journal to Stella*, ed. F. Ryland (1900)
103. *Sydenham, Forest Hill, and Penge Gazette* (1873–1965)
104. Thorne, James, *Handbook to the Environs of London* (1876)
105. Timpson, Thomas, *Church History of Kent* (1859)
106. Van Lokeren, A., *Chartes et documents de l'Abbaye de Saint Pierre au mont Blandin à Gand* (1868–71)
107. Wallenberg, J.K., *The Place-Names of Kent* (1934)
108. Werner, Alexander, 'Thomas Betts, an Eighteenth Century Glasscutter' *Journal of the Glass Association,* vol. I (1985)
109. Wesley, John, *Journals* (1836)
110. White, Ken, *The Public Houses of Lee and Lewisham* (1992)
111. Wilberforce, Robert and Samuel, *The Life of William Wilberforce* (1838)
112. Witney, K.P., *The Kingdom of Kent* (1982)

Acknowledgements

Most of the illustrations in this volume are from originals at the Lewisham Local History Centre, and I am grateful to the London Borough of Lewisham for permission to reproduce them. A number of others are from the Martin Collection at the Greenwich Local History Library. I have to thank Mr Julian Watson, the Librarian, for help in locating these valuable drawings and prints, and Mr Neil Rhind, the Martin trustee, for allowing me to use them. The pictures in question are those on pages 30 and 104, the top one on page 48, both paintings on page 106, and the frontispiece.

Mr Rhind was also kind enough to read through the Blackheath sections of the text and to save me from many blunders. Mr Ken George willingly put his vast knowledge of local cinemas at my disposal, and Mr Michael Egan, the historian of Kidbrooke, drew my attention to some valuable Lewisham sources. Mr Godfrey Smith, whose work on Hither Green is keenly awaited, has generously shared his many discoveries with me – discoveries that range far wider than the history of Hither Green.

The charming watercolour of The Wood is from the Devonshire Collection at Chatsworth, and is reproduced by kind permission of the Chatsworth Settlement Trustees. My thanks to Mr John Kenworthy-Browne for informing me of its existence, and to Mr Michael Pearmen, the Librarian and Archivist at Chatsworth, for providing me with a copy.

I am extremely grateful to Dr A.S. Morgan for permitting me to reproduce the artist's impression of Granville Park from the original in his possession. Bringing this rare print to my notice is one of the many contributions made to the book by Mr Stephen Moreton Prichard. He has also copied and printed most of the illustrations – some from highly unpromising paintings and drawings – and provided the cover photograph.

I am greatly indebted to Professor Bernard Bergonzi for permission to quote some lines from *Victorian Houses, Sydenham Hill*. They first appeared in his *Descartes and the Animals: Poems, 1948–1954* (Platform, 1954).

Index

Adams, William Dacres, 53
Alfred, King, 2
Allen family, 46, 57
alsmhouses, 13, 23, 30, 90–1, 97
Armoury Mill, 28, 41, 42

Bampton, Robert of, 4–5
Batchelor, John, 20–1
Bell Green, 16, 47, 64, 79, 81, 95
Bellingham, 1, 5, 76, 93, 94, 97
Black Death, 8–9
black immigration, 31–2
Blackheath, 7, 9, 11, 12, 25–6, 29, 32, 33, 34, 38–40, 46–7, 51, 52, 53–4, 97, 107–10
Blackheath church, 53–4, 69
Blackheath Fair, 25, 26, 34, 108
Blackwell, Ebenezer, 32–3, 37
bomb damage, 92, 97, 105
Bowdler, Thomas, 54
bridges, 13, 35, 36, 37, 56, 106
Brockley, 1, 5, 7, 17, 56, 57
Brockley Hall, 96
Brockley Jack, the, 86
Bromley Hill House, 49
building societies, 61
bull baiting, 42

Cade, Jack, 11
cage, 105
Campbell, Thomas, 45, 53
Caroline, Princes of Wales, 39–40
Catford, 2, 5, 9, 10, 13, 17, 35, 60, 81
Catford Bridge, 35
Catford Conservative Club *see* Elmwood
Catford House, 49, 50
cemeteries, 68
Cheseman family, 16
Chiesman Brothers, 63, 86
Church House, 6
Church of the Ascension *see* Dartmouth chapel
cinemas, 82, 84, 96, 97
clerks, 81, 96
Cole, James, 66, 68
Colfe, Abraham, 14–16, 19–23
Colfe's Almshouses, 23, 90–1
Colfe's English School, 23, 73
Colfe's Grammar School 22–3, 37–8, 73, 84, 107
Colfe's Library, 23, 73
College Farm, 62
Congregational churches, 25, 52, 69, 85, 103
Constable, Abraham, 51, 62
Corbett, Archibald Cameron, 79
Corbett Estate, 79–80, 81–2
crime, 7–8, 32, 48–9, 52, 68–9, 81–2, 105
Crofton Park *see* Brockley
Croydon Canal, 45, 56–7
Crystal Palace, 60, 61, 69–72

Dartmouth, barons and earls of 19, 25–6, 33, 34, 37, 46–7, 54–4, 60, 69, 74, 88, 90
Dartmouth chapel, 26, 40–1, 74, 107
Dartmouth Grove, 108

Dartmouth Hill, 109
Dartmouth House, 107
Dartmouth Point, 53, 107
Dartmouth Row, 25–6, 33, 52, 107–9
Davies, Methusalem, 40, 50, 103
Deptford, 11, 27, 52, 93, 99–100
Dermody, Thomas, 45
Dickens, Charles, 38, 59
Domesday Book, 3–4
Downham, 93–4, 97
Duncan, Leland Lewis, 3, 4, 6, 90, 111
Dunstan, Archbishop, 2

Edgar, King, 1, 2
electricity, 81, 96
Elfrida, 2
Eliot family *see* St Germans
Eliot Place, 39
Elizabeth I, 12–14
Elmwood, 34, 47, 79, 90
enclosures, 14–15, 25–6, 41, 45–9, 105
entertainments, 49–52, 69, 83–4
Evelyn, John, 22, 23, 26, 34

Fairlawn Park, 79
farming, 10, 14, 18–19, 76, 91
Flower House Estate, 98
Forest Hill, 39, 45, 47–9, 58, 70–2
Forest Hill Industrial Homes, 72–3
Forster family, 35, 46, 49, 53, 65–6, 76, 80, 91
Fox's Fields, 43–4

gas, 67
Gaumont Palace cinema, 97
George public house, 20, 55
German church, Forest Hill, 71
German immigrants, 71, 95

Ghent *see* St Peter's
Gibson, George, 37, 38, 39, 61, 108, 110
Glynn, John, 14
Grace, W.G., 83
Grahme, Raynold or Reginals, 19
Grahme, Susannah, 26, 74
Granville Park, 60, 61, 110
Green Man, Blackheath, 26, 52, 109
Greenwich, 2, 3, 4, 6, 8, 9, 11, 12, 28, 51
Grove, Sir George, 71
Grove House, 40, 57, 59, 105

Hammet, Sir Benjamin, 40, 41
Hare and Billet, the, 39
Hatcliffe, William, 11, 45
health, 18, 30–1, 44, 64, 67–8, 82
Henry V, 10, 11
Henry VIII, 12, 13
Hether Grove Estate, 98
High Pavement, the, 62–3, 105
Hither Green, 5, 8–9, 16, 28, 39, 46, 62, 79–80, 81, 82
Hollyband, Claudius, 4
Home and Infirmary for Sick Children, 68
Honor Oak Estate, 97–8
Honor Oak Hill, 13
Honor Oak Road, 13, 39, 45
Horniman, Frederick John, 71, 83
hospitals, 30, 68, 72, 82, 89
housing, 41, 43–4, 57, 58–62, 75, 77–80, 92–4, 96–8
How, Ephraim, 29
hunting, 49–50

industry, 28–9, 41–3, 76, 81–2

James I, 13, 14, 15, 17
Jutes, 1

Kent Waterworks, 49, 64
Knoll, the, 39, 61, 110

Ladywell, 5, 41, 50, 60, 68, 79, 88, 89–90
Ladywell Bridge, 36
Lawrie Park, 45, 50, 71
Lee, 4, 5, 14, 89, 100
Lee, John and Henry, 42, 98
Legge, Augustus, 77–8
Legge, Edward, 46, 53
Legge family *see also* Dartmouth
Legge, Henry, 54, 65, 73, 77
Legh, Edward, 59, 65, 73
Lewisham Antiquarian Society, 90
Lewisham Board of Works, 64, 65–7, 77, 87–9
Lewisham Bridge, 13, 37, 105–7
Lewisham Bridge Mill, 28, 29
Lewisham Clock Tower, frontispiece, 48–9, 88, 105
Lewisham High Street, passim
Lewisham Hill, 9, 22, 105, 107
Lewisham Hippodrome, 84
Lewisham House, 38, 87, 90, 103
Lewisham, London Borough, 99–100
Lewisham, Metropolitan Borough, 89–90, 93–4, 97–9
Lewisham Nursery, 28, 62
Lewisham Park, 16, 60
Lewisham Priory, 4, 5–6
Lewisham School, 38
Lewisham station, 59–60
Lewisham Town Hall, 66, 87–8
Lewisham Union, 44
Lewisham Vestry, 65, 66, 73
Limes, the, 32–3, 59, 90, 104–5
Loat's Pits, 43
local government, 65–8, 87–90, 99–100
London and Croydon Railway, 45, 58–9
London Road, Forest Hill, 58, 87
Long, Charles, Lord Farnborough, 49
Lowth, William, 33, 40

Manns, August, 71
manor courts, 6–7, 65
manors, 5, 9, 10
Marryat, Captain Frederick, 47
Marryat, Joseph, 47
Mayow, Mary, 45, 53, 54
Mayow, Mayow Wynell, 46
Methodism, 32–3, 52–3, 69, 85
moats, 5, 10
Molesworth Street, 60, 104
Montpelier Row, 39
Morden Hill, 7, 52, 82, 107
Morton, Joshua, 40–1, 109
Mount Pleasant House, 62

Nash, Edwin, 71
New Cross Turnpike Trust, 27, 61, 66
Noakes family, 96

Paganini, Niccolo, 52
Pagoda, the, 40
Paragon, the, 39
parks, 83
parliamentary elections, 90, 94, 99, 100
Paxton, Sir Joseph, 70–2
Peasants' Revolt, the, 9
Penge, 89
Perceval House, 33–4, 74, 108
Perry Hill, 16, 23, 36
Perry Vale, 45, 46
Peter, John, 25
Place House, 9
place names, 1–2
plague, 18

Plough, the, 34, 59
Plough Green, 47
police, 30, 52, 68
population, 4, 18, 31, 44, 60, 70, 76, 91, 94, 99
poverty, 29–31, 41–3, 44–5, 74–5, 81, 95–6, 100
Prendergast, Joseph, 73
Prendergast's School, 84
Priory Farm, 6, 10
Priory, the, 49, 55, 65, 78
Priory *see also* Lewisham Priory
public baths, 87–8
public houses, 19–20, 21, 25, 26, 32, 50, 85–6
public libraries, 23, 73, 83

railways, 45, 58–60, 76
Ravensbourne Park, 35, 49–50, 57
Ravensbourne River, 1, 28, 64
Riverdale Mill, 28, 104
Roebuck, the 50, 60, 105–7
Roman Catholic Church, 85
Romans, 1
Romborough, 8–9
Romborough Way Estate, 93, 97, 101
Rookery, the, 28, 32, 58, 103
Rosentha, 49, 55, 67, 78, 90
Rushey Green, 47, 64–5
Rushey Green Place, 10, 11, 15, 17

St Bartholomew's church, 53–4, 68, 73
St Bartholomew's National Schools, 54–5
St Dunstan's College, 84–5
St Germans, earls of, 39, 46, 60, 79
St Mary's church, 1, 3, 9, 13–14, 20, 27, 32, 37–8, 54, 66, 68, 77, 101
St Mary's National Schools, 36, 66, 101
St Mary's, Sydenham Hill, 98
St Mary's Vicarage, 14, 26, 27, 40, 103
St Matthew's, 73
St Peter's Abbey, Ghent, 2–10, 12
St Philip's, 71
St Stephen's, 69, 105
Saravia, Adrian de, 14
schools, 14, 16, 22–3, 27, 37–9, 40, 41, 54–5, 73, 84–5
Second World War, 92, 96–7
sewers, 62–5
Shaw, George Bernard, 85
Shene Priory, 11–12, 16
shops, 62–3, 65–6, 85–7, 96, 98
Silk Mills *see* Armoury Mill
Slum clearance, 96
smallpox, 44
Smiles, Samuel, 60, 83, 110
Smith, James, 7, 52
South field, 16
Southend chapel, 53
Southend Hall, 35, 91, 96
Southend village, 17, 27, 29, 36, 53, 57, 91, 98
Sparrow, Jane, 32
sport, 49–51, 82–3, 109
Springfield, 55, 64–5, 78
Stainton, Henry, 55, 64–5
Stanhope, George, 26–8, 29
Stanhope's school for girls, 27
Stanstead Road, 61, 64, 79
stocks, 48–9
Stoddard, Sir Nicholas, 6, 16
Stone, Sapientia, 33, 39, 74
Streete House, 40, 101–2
Swift, Jonathan, 26–7, 103
Sydenham, 1–2, 5, 9, 13, 14–15, 16–17, 18, 23–5, 34, 36, 38, 39, 45–9, 50, 53–5, 56–7, 58,

63–4, 68, 69–73, 79, 80, 81, 83, 84, 86, 88, 95, 97, 98
Sydenham Bridge, 56–7
Sydenham Children's Hospital *see* Home and Infirmary for Sick Children
Sydenham Fair, 34
Sydenham Park, 58
Sydenham Wells, 23–5

tanning, 28
Tetley family, 71
Thackeray, John, 30, 55, 65, 78
Thackeray's Almshouses, 30
theatres, 51, 84
'Thorpe' Estate, Sydenham, 80
trams, 76–7, 80, 90, 91, 93
Tyler, Wat, 9

Union Chapel, 52

Vulliamy, Lewis, 54

Watch House Green, 47–9, 105
water mills, 3, 28–9, 35, 42, 91
water supply, 49, 64
Wells Park Road, 23–5, 49
Wesley, John and Charles, 32–3
West Kent Park, 61
Westwood Common, 13, 14–15, 23–5, 34, 45–9
whipping post, 48–9
Whitefield, George, 32
Whitefield's Mount, 12, 32
Whitworth, Benjamin, 90
Wilkes, John, 40
Williams, Theophilus William, 88–9
Wilson, George, 51
Wire, David Williams, 65
Wood, the, 71–2
woodlands, 1, 10, 16, 18–19
workhouses, 29–30, 41, 43, 44–5, 68, 74–5, 82, 89–90